More Praise for Double the

"Reading this book is like having Li_____dom and whispering her secrets in your _____ ____ate you from the start; lead you through a m_____ ____ice, and workshop activities; and leave you wondering how quickly you can implement one of her brilliant ideas. Lisa is the consummate story teller who combines real-world recommendations with wit and humor, leaving you laughing, reflecting, and wanting more."
—**Elaine Biech, author of** *The Business of Consulting* **and editor of** *The ASTD Leadership Handbook*

"Lisa has unlocked the secrets of the push and pull of engagement and accountability at work. She offers stories, guidance, and insights to find the healthy push and pull of work to "double the love" as we race toward a 2020 workplace. You will love this book and the results and relationship building it offers you at work."
—**David Zinger, David Zinger Associates, founder and host of 6,300-member Employee Engagement Network**

"A truly fantastic book. Engagement really is about making work meaningful and purposeful."
—**Lloyd Lopez, Supervisor of Client Services, Quest Diagnostics**

"Outstanding! A terrific fun-to-read book that provides clear steps for organizational excellence."
— **Martin D. Moll, Practice Leader, AKT CPAs and Business Consultants**

"I absolutely love that I can grab this amazing book, apply the tools, and be inspired to make my work world a better place. *Double the Love* left me feeling engaged and empowered! Lisa's "20 Ways to Be an Advocate" are great reminders of how easy it is to make someone's day and build a relationship."
—**Johna Campbell, Senior Manager of HR, Kollmorgen**

"If you want to transform your teams and help them perform better, you need to know the secrets in two areas: accountability and engagement. Thankfully, this book focuses on simple (though not always easy) ways you can double your love and thus double your results. Lisa not only shares the secrets but teaches you how to use them to do more and to maximize the performance of your team. Believe it: You *can* double the love!"
—**Phil Gerbyshak, author, speaker, and VP of Sales and Marketing, Advisology**

"Those who treasure Lisa's practical, humorous, and popular books will love her mind-bending secrets that lead people just as they are. Expect to spot *cranky, courageous,* and *creative* under refreshing new lights. Her leadership words of wisdom come chock full of passion and the kinds of tools and skills workers crave. Lisa Haneberg is clearly at her best in this book!"
—**Ellen Weber (PhD), Innovation Director, Mita International Brain Center**

"In *Double the Love*, Lisa Haneberg has written a book that redefines accountability and engagement systems for each of us who need to be able to bring out the very best in people. She includes assessments, exercises, and other tools that are guaranteed to move you along the continuum to more effective leadership—wherever you may be today. Her content and writing style make it a must read."
—**Brenda Gumbs, EVP of Human Resources, Perfetti Van Melle, USA, Inc.**

"*Double the Love* is a treasure trove of transformative ideas, secrets, and wisdom on how to build an engaged and accountable workforce. Wish I had this book early on when I built my first team!"
—**Tanmay Vora, author, blogger, and improvement consultant, QAspire.com**

"Accountability is one of the most lip-serviced words on the planet, but Lisa changes the game of accountability in *Double the Love.* Want a powerful team? Want to be a great leader? Read this book and change your world!"
—**Dwayne Melancon, Chief Technology Officer, Tripwire, Inc., and author of GenuineCuriosity.com**

"Zounds! After breakthroughs, the "secrets" were always right there in our face. Leadership that is intentional, persistent, yet humble and lovingly refocusing the "me" to the "we"—sounds like the team I want to be on."
—**Jeff Krida, Vice Chairman & Co-founder, American Queen Steamboat Company**

"Extra love doesn't cost you anything, so why don't more leaders give it away? *Double the Love* will give you the must-have tools to deliver better results, get promoted faster, and inspire others to do it too!"
—**Cory Bouck, Director of Organizational Development & Learning, Johnsonville Sausage, and author of *The Lens of Leadership***

"When it comes to understanding what makes people feel truly engaged in their work, no one cuts through the clutter of organizational improvement processes, tools, and other assorted junk, and gets quicker to the heart of what really matters than Lisa Haneberg. In her new book *Double the Love*, Lisa provides a set of simple secrets that will help you more effectively develop highly accountable and engaged teams within your organization."
—**Chris Grams, President, New Kind**

"Lisa brings a wealth of personal experience and knowledge to the table in this book. A refreshing and honest look at improving dynamics within your team that I highly recommend to anyone hoping to bring a new level of excellence to the workplace."
—**David Loewe, Chief Executive Officer, Seattle Humane Society**

"If you want better business results, open your mind, a good bottle of red, and read *Double the Love*. Haneberg guides with her unique mix of wit, big experience, and perspective in a way that challenges leaders' beliefs and actions about accountability and the holy grail of discretionary effort."
—**Randy Boek, Professional Outsider and President, Route Two**

"With her usual playful style, Lisa has once again delivered an accessible yet hard-hitting take on some of the biggest challenges facing leaders today. Striking the right balance between accountability and engagement is an art form. Haneberg serves up a thought-provoking primer on the theory behind her 11 secrets for building strong teams and a practical field guide for how to bring these ideas to life. I already found three things I'm planning to try at work on Monday!"
—**Kathleen Goodman, Director of Strategy, Planning, and Management, Bill & Melinda Gates Foundation**

"Lisa's insights on accountability, engagement, and LOVE will forever change the way you view the performance management process. She has managed to, once again, clearly communicate the critical information that will project you and your team to levels you never thought possible."
—**Karin Rasmusson, SPHR, HR Results**

DOUBLE

The LOVE

11 Secrets for
Cultivating Highly Accountable
and Engaged Teams

Lisa Haneberg

TPH
Trainers Publishing House
Fairfax, Virginia

Trainers Publishing House
www.trainerspublishinghouse.com
Email: info@trainerspublishinghouse.com

Ordering Information

Quantity Sales: sales@trainerspublishinghouse.com
Individual Sales: Amazon.com and Kindle.com

Library of Congress Control Number: 2014935729
ISBN: 978-1-93924-704-9 (print)
ISBN: 978-1-93924-705-6 (Kindle)

TPH Editorial Team:

Publisher/Editor: Cat Russo
Editorial Manager: Jacqueline Edlund-Braun
Rights Associate and Data Manager: Nancy Silva
Communication Specialist: Stephanie Sussan
Writer/editor: Tora Estep
Design and Composition: Debra Deysher, Double D Media
Marketing: Dawn Baron, Passion Profits Consulting

Cover and text design by Debra Deysher
Cover art by zmkstudio, Shutterstock

Contents

INTRODUCTION

The Secret Path to Excellence

Everybody loves a secret. We pull our heads together close as our minds spin in anticipation. What's she going to say? What will it mean? Is the secret upbeat and positive, or deep and dark? Secrets tap into and reach different parts of our brain than do everyday suggestions. The notion of a secret makes the conversation instantly more intriguing and enticing. This is a book of secrets.

Is this just hype or a ruse to compel your attention? No! Leadership is all about helping people do their best work, and people are strange and mysterious creatures. There are many secrets to uncover! I will share 11 secrets with you gleaned from my more than 25 years of leading teams, training leaders, and writing about leading. Some of these secrets will make you think "ooh, cool!" and others might make you feel uneasy. All have the potential to be game changers. Really! Here's how I define a *secret*:

- Insights and wisdom most people don't know or haven't heard, or if they have, they've buried it deep inside where it's tough to access

- Common sense that we don't commonly practice or is made inert by unintentionally phony practices

- Revelations that are counterintuitive

- Intertwined ideas that most of us have never connected before

These 11 secrets will help you catalyze excellence. Optimizing performance is our prime directive, right? It's the reason we exist as leaders and managers. We choose to lead so we can make the big plays and facilitate positive change. Our organizations ache for this, and we know it happens when our team members bring their A+ game to work—when everyone's efforts are focused, innovative, and driven. I call this ideal way of working *performance velocity* because we want our teams to perform with speed (movement, progress) and direction (on path, creative, focused, working on what most matters).

The secrets cluster around two leadership systems that we use every day and that support performance velocity: accountability and engagement. Our workplaces are abuzz with the terms, our goals are dotted with them, and our development plans address how we can get better at leading more engaged and accountable teams. Of all the training courses I offer, my session called "Accountability and Engagement" is the most popular and most requested. And when I talk about the two terms in the same sentence, people commonly nod and respond with something like, "Ooh, yeah, we need more of that."

It is precisely because of this interest that I can bring this book of secrets to you, my dear readers. I have been teaching, coaching, researching, and exploring all things accountability and engagement so much over the last several years that it is like breathing to me. I have seen the approaches that work—and those that are nothing more than slick window dressing. Fads? Oh, golly, there are hundreds of accountability or engagement systems you can buy and use. Eager consultants hoping to attract new clients or a sweet speaking gig in Fiji or Bruges publish thousands of books, many with accompanying videos you can buy for $99. (Now, you might be thinking, "Wait a minute, Lisa, aren't you a consultant with a book and wouldn't you go to Fiji if I paid you to?" Technically, I am no longer a consultant—I have a real day job—but you're right, I would gladly go to Fiji or Bruges!)

Somehow I got off my point . . . which was . . . ah, yes, I have been breathing this stuff and have distilled what I have learned to share these secrets with you. It is not a system, there are no licensing fees, and I won't ask you to join my subscription membership (my publisher is reading this thinking, "Well don't count anything out, Lisa . . ." Funny!). I will, however, ask you to consider these 11 secrets with an open mind and an interested heart. If you do, amazing things will happen. I know it. You can send me a nasty email if they don't, but only *after* you read Section I of the book in its entirety.

It is important that we explore and challenge the practices we rely on to enhance accountability and engagement. The stakes are high—we are dealing with people's careers and our organization's success. We need to move beyond defining best practices as "the things that big *Fortune* 500 organizations do." Many well-respected companies of all sizes are struggling with how to bring out the very best in people.

So despite our understanding that engagement is a critical element in organization success, our well-intended efforts to engage employees often do the opposite. We know this—our organizations know this (yes, I just anthropomorphized the "organization," but let's face it, they behave like creatures)—and yet we stay the course. Do we honestly think that free cupcakes and printed mouse pads make people want to try harder? They are surface-level gimmicks at best. We also instantly recognize that precious moment when a leader says something extraordinary that truly moves the audience—now that's a beautiful thing.

If your doctor told you that there was no evidence that a certain drug would help you lower your sky-high blood pressure but you should take it anyway because it's well known and all the rage, would you do it? If you answered "yes," step away from the book and go have a cupcake or two. I cannot help you.

Sorry . . . . I shouldn't be so blunt.

I still can't help you.

Still here? Awesome. Here's the point. We know that many of the things that we do in hopes of increasing engagement don't work. We know this, and it's frustrating. But the great news is that there are ways to inspire life, spark, and drive in our teams, and it is possible to make a real and positive impact on employee engagement.

In the same spirit, it is healthy to challenge our approaches to increasing *accountability* as well. Accountability is something we do to people. Its seed comes from scientific management (command and control) and industrial management techniques. Accountability is not empowerment (don't get me started on why empowerment is just another word for "I am still in charge, hah!"). We can try to call it something more enlightened, but we would be wrong. And we would look dumb. The ways we approach accountability are screaming for some get-real conversations, and we will have them here in this book.

Based on the preceding mini-rant, you might think I am suggesting that accountability and engagement are bad things to want (and that I hate cupcakes, neither of which is true). In fact, I think both accountability and engagement are essential for creating performance velocity. It's the *ways* many of us and our organizations try to increase accountability and engagement that I want to challenge and improve. This is where the secrets come in. And this is what the book will be: a no BS zone of real talk about how we can make the greatest possible difference as leaders.

Looking up at that last paragraph it occurs to me that it sounds a bit bloated—as if I think I know something that most leaders don't and therefore am enlightened. Hmmmm . . . . how to handle . . . . I don't feel that I know and that you do not. In fact, I am sure the secrets are alive and well deep inside you. *I think you know all of it.* Many of us, however, have been conditioned away from what our instincts would tell us by slickly presented, well-intended systems that lead us off track. The snow-balling, butterfly-flapping, accumulating effect is not good. So, I am not better or smarter, but I do feel freer, perhaps, and more comfortable in my shoes as a leader to give those little voices in my head some airtime to challenge the status quo.

After 25 years in the field of leadership and leadership training, I have never been more fascinated by what's possible than I am now. Constructively cynical? Yes. Blown away by what's possible? Double yes.

In Section I, I lay the overall foundation for the book and share the 11 secrets. We live in a TED Talk, YouTube, Instagram world, and this is my narrative equivalent. It's the keynote speech of the book. The manifesto. In this section I hope to pique your interest and leave you feeling motivated to tweak your leadership practices.

In Section II, the "Workshop," I will help you discover how to put the 11 secrets into practice. I will share examples and tools to help you see the ideas in action, so you can hone in on what you can do differently next Tuesday at two o'clock.

Please join me in my quest to proliferate these secrets for cultivating excellence. I have been observing leaders for a long time and am clearer now more than ever about what distinguishes the best from those who struggle and drive us batty. If I were Oprah, I would say: "This is what I know for sure." So, lean in close . . . I have a secret to share.

SECTION ONE

The Keynote

The Keynote and Introduction to the Accountability and Engagement Model

People are amazing. And cranky. And courageous. And fearful. And unpredictable. And funny. And stuck in a rut. And driven to be great. Highly talented and deeply flawed. Tough to manage, but easy to love. Motivational fires on Monday become a burnout scene on Thursday. Nothing is the same except our changing proclivities to nurture, surprise, delight, and frustrate others—all during a one-hour meeting! People are complex and amazing, and I bet that this is why you became a leader.

This is a book about catalyzing peoples' greatness so that it serves a big purpose. I believe that everyone wants to make a difference even if today they are inert (that is, slow or unable to act). I believe that as leaders we all feel a passion for progress. And I love how we light up, inside and out, when our efforts change people's lives for the better.

The 11 secrets came about over time and represent essential ideas about leading people and creating performance velocity (performing with speed and focus). Each secret was revealed to me as I worked with leaders throughout my career (learning from both the great and the lousy!). I feel lucky to have uncovered the secrets (and am even more lucky to use them as part of my leadership practices). I look forward to sharing them with you.

Accountability and Engagement Systems Defined

Before I describe the secrets, though, it's important to clarify what we mean by accountability and engagement. As I am using the terms, *accountability* and *engagement* are two distinct management systems.

The Accountability and Engagement Model shown in Figure 1.1 offers a simple illustration of the two systems.

Figure 1.1 Accountability and Engagement Model

Managers hold people accountable.

Associated with Scientific Management
Extrinsic Motivation

People choose to engage.

Associated with Intrinsic Motivation
Ownership

Accountability

An accountability system is used to ensure that all employees understand what their managers expect from them, what excellence looks like in action, how they are performing, and when and how they need to adjust work practices. Leaders hold employees accountable. They do this through a system of actions:

- Clarifying and aligning roles—ensuring that the right people are doing the right work

- Defining, communicating, and describing expectations so that all employees know what excellence looks like in terms of performance and behaviors

- Providing timely, candid, and clear feedback about how employees are performing

- Measuring work and processes against the highest priority goals (great metrics tell people the score)

- Evaluating employees periodically to give them a good picture for their overall contributions to the organization and to define development plan goals

- Rewarding performance and outcomes that are in alignment with expectations and definitions of excellence

- Recognizing great effort and work, including excellence in teaming and collaboration

- Providing meaningful consequences for performance that fails to meet standards

If you have an accountability problem, or feel that there is a lack of accountability, realize that the focus should be on improving managerial practices and follow-through. I am not saying that you are the problem . . . well, actually I kind of am. If you have an accountability problem, you have a management problem. But you can fix it!

Engagement

Ironically, when some leaders say they want more accountability, what they mean is that they want their employees to show more ownership or engagement in their work. But engagement is a very different thing and is not something that leaders can demand— employees choose whether to engage in their work, their department's goals, and their organization's mission. Leaders, however, can create a work environment that improves the likelihood of high employee engagement, and the best leaders do this very well.

Engagement happens when employees give discretionary effort and 100 percent to a task. These moments transcend the basic employee– employer relationship and show a higher level of connection and commitment. You cannot force engagement to happen, but you can build a culture where it is more likely to flourish. Elements of the ideal environment for engagement include the following:

- Challenging work and interesting problems to solve.

- Connection to the work, the team, and the industry/ organization. Stronger connections bring people together.

- A feeling of being cared for. Leaders who show they care and make their employees feel special and valued will earn more employee ownership.

- Collaboration and partnership. When people work together to seize an opportunity or solve a problem, they tend to engage and feel more pride for their work (increasing connection too).

- Opportunities to grow as a person and as a professional. Your employees want to feel as if they are expanding their skills and staying up-to-date in their chosen field.

- Autonomy to make choices that affect their work.

- A feeling that their work has meaning and is important to the organization.

- Work and workplaces that are fun and lighthearted.

If you have an engagement problem, or feel that there is a lack of employee engagement, realize that the focus should be on igniting intrinsic motivation.

Accountability and Engagement Differentiated

Looking at the Accountability and Engagement Model presented in Figure 1.1, think about the jobs you have held throughout your career and whether each work environment seemed stronger in accountability or in engagement. Both are critical for success. Both are important. But the managerial practices that strengthen one might not be the same as those that build the other—in fact, it is unlikely.

This last point is a key learning and important to restate. Accountability and engagement are different and are supported through unique managerial practices. It is possible, and very common, that you are a bit lopsided in your approach—favoring either accountability or engagement practices. Organizations also tend to emphasize one environment more than the other.

Here is another way to think about the difference between accountability and engagement: Accountability is a "push" system; engagement is a "pull" system. When we hold someone accountable, we are the ones in charge and calling the shots. We are *pushing* expectations and consequences to our employees. When it comes to engagement, however, employees are the ones in control and calling the shots. Our practices as leaders, then, must *pull* them in or they won't work. This important distinction hints at why the practices that reinforce each system are different. We will explore the push and pull idea much more throughout the book.

> *Accountability is a "push" system; engagement is a "pull" system.*

Accountability, Engagement, and the 11 Secrets

I have shared this model of accountability and engagement with thousands of leaders, and it tends to resonate with them. And as is the case with all good models, this one provokes questions: How does this work? Why does this work? What does this really mean? The secrets revealed in this book add depth to the model while answering some of these questions. Here are the 11 secrets for building highly accountable and engaged teams:

1. Using accountability systems to produce excellence is like taking a pocket knife to a gun fight.

2. To make accountability systems work, you may need to double the love.

3. Droning accountability measures and goals into people's heads puts them to sleep.

4. The secret to accountability is grit.

5. The secret to engagement is managerial love.

6. Engagement is a gift you might not have earned.

7. Your most talented, highest performing, employees might also be your least engaged.

8. You have a secret weapon you can use to engage others.

9. Surveys matter when you love lower scores more than higher ones.

10. Most managers think time is precious but behave like it is worthless.

11. The secret to performance velocity is design.

Secrets 1–4 relate to accountability, Secrets 5–8 address engagement, and Secrets 9–11 apply to both.

Armed with the model and the secrets, you will be ready to hone your leadership practices to cultivate excellence and build performance velocity in your teams. Let's dig into the secrets, shall we?

CHAPTER ONE

Choose the Right Tools

The Four Questions

As an introduction to the first secret, I will tell you about an exercise that I have facilitated dozens of times during management training sessions and that often blows the minds of my participants (in a good way!). It is deceptively simple and goes like this. I divide the class into four groups and ask each group to answer one question on a piece of flip chart paper. Each group only sees the question they have been asked to answer. After 10 minutes, each group reveals their question and their responses. Here are the questions, in the order I ask the groups to reveal their answers:

1. How would you define *results orientation*?

2. What does *results orientation* look like in action?

3. How can leaders *best* help people do their best work?

4. What has your leader done that most helped you do your best work?

The first two questions are similar, and the answers are predictable. Groups mention actions such as setting expectations, measuring performance, managing performance, giving feedback, following through on deadlines, and communicating progress. There is little variability in how groups define *results orientation*. And most leaders are aware of the term because many of their organizations select it as a management competency. Question 2 responses tend to be a bit more thoughtful because it is harder to answer and requires group members to imagine results orientation in action. Even so, the responses to question 2 overlap almost completely with those of question 1.

After the first two groups present, participants from these groups seem unimpressed and are probably wondering if the entire class is going to be this lame. But hold on, the second two questions have yet to be revealed!

I ask the groups assigned questions 3 and 4 to share their questions and responses. As with the first two questions, these questions are similar and the answers are predictable. Common responses include coaching, spending time, giving a challenge, showing they care, removing roadblocks, being an inspiration, and listening. At this point in the exercise, participants are a bit curious about the questions but might be wondering why I am getting paid to stand up and tell them what's obvious.

It's time for the mind-blowing part.

At its core, we would have to conclude that results orientation is about achieving results. Great results. To be results oriented, therefore, leaders need to do whatever it takes to produce the best possible results. Right?

The class agrees. This is right.

To get the best possible results, people need to do their best work. Right?

Right. Heads nodding. Minds starting to buzz.

But you all just said that the things leaders do that enable employees to do their best work are different than what leaders do when they are being results oriented. What gives?

They are all looking at me, not sure what to say but seeing that something is wonky about this.

This exercise reveals a common problem of definition. Most organizations talk about the importance of being results oriented and most define it far too narrowly to be useful. If the actions that leaders can take to enable employees to do their best work (and thereby get the best results) are those types of things that you listed for questions 3 and

4, then these would need to be included in our definition of results orientation, right?

Right. All agree.

How we define things matters, and you can imagine how things might be different if we used a more complete and correct definition of results orientation. Our goals would look different, our performance evaluations would focus on different things, our coaching would be different, and our hiring criteria would be different.

At this point, I usually begin to see proverbial light bulbs turning on, and we continue to discuss what this insight means for how they will manage in the future. There are two recommendations that come from this exercise:

- Realize that how we traditionally define results orientation is incomplete and that the actions we typically associate with results orientation are limited in their ability to produce great results. It's ironic but true. Don't expect these managerial practices to do more than they are designed to do.

- Redefine what it means to be results oriented to include managerial practices that enable and encourage employees to do their best work. Re-imagine how you should best spend your time based on this expanded definition.

I share this activity with you at the beginning of this book because I think it highlights an important mistake that many of us make and that we need to correct before we explore accountability and engagement further. The mistake is asking a system designed to encourage compliance-level performance to produce excellence-level performance. Let me explain.

Questions 1 and 2 asked about results orientation. Questions 3 and 4 focused on enabling employees to do their best work. While there are actions that occasionally show up on both sets of questions, the answers are consistently unique between the two sets. And if you have not already figured this out, the results-orientation questions describe accountability practices and the best work questions describe engagement practices. Almost never are the accountability practices listed as ones that enable best performance. Are they needed? Yes. Do they make me want to do amazing things? Hardly.

Here's the crux of it. Accountability systems, which are managerial practices that increase accountability, are not capable of producing excellence. Even the best accountability systems are not designed to do this. This insight is so important that it bears repeating: Accountability systems are not designed to produce excellence. That said, our workplaces need accountability, so please don't interpret that I am saying accountability is not important—after all, half of this book is dedicated to accountability. But I do want to make sure that you know what the utility of this system is and is not. We need highly accountable teams. We also need policies. And safety guidelines. And clear job descriptions. All of these are compliance-oriented systems.

> *The mistake is asking a system designed to encourage compliance-level performance to produce excellence-level performance.*

Beyond accountability, however, our organizations should also inspire new thinking. And high levels of collaboration. And a yearning to learn. And a sense of unity and purpose. And a drive for excellence. But let's be clear, accountability systems do not produce this second set of workplace conditions. Accountability is more like a policy manual for performance.

SECRET 1: Using accountability systems to produce excellence is like taking a pocket knife to a gun fight. *Choose the right tools.*

This is the first secret because the idea is fundamental and will impact how we look at accountability from here forward. Accountability is a good thing and important to an organization's success, but accountability alone will not produce excellence.

The next secret we look at, **Secret 2**, addresses how accountability measures can inadvertently muck with other aspects of the work environment.

Counterbalance the Crud of Change

The Bloodbankers

As a consultant, I worked on a lot of team angst issues. It became a bit of a specialty, largely because organizations often don't know what to do when hard-working, dedicated, long-term employees start getting snarky with one another. One such project involved a team in a large health-care system in the Midwest. They all worked in the blood bank, and most on the team had been there for many years. The head of human resources (HR) said that the team members came down to her office to complain about their manager. I will call her Joy. Basically, the team threw Joy under the bus and said they didn't want to work for her. The HR leader and the functional director (to whom the manager reported) were surprised by the team's complaints and asked me to determine what was going on and what should be done about it (including whether Joy should be let go or demoted).

I can remember thinking that Joy must have done something pretty bad to provoke a group of people to march down to HR and lodge a complaint. And I wondered how she was handling all this, especially knowing that an outside consultant had been called to do an investigation.

I interviewed each of the "bloodbankers" (what they called themselves) individually for 90 minutes. I also talked to Joy, the functional director, and the HR leader. I asked about what things were like within the team and department, whether anything had changed, about how the team works, and about Joy's management style and practices. I was warned that no one would talk to me, but nearly everyone was quite open. They were also incredibly emotional! One older team member cried because she felt personally attacked by Joy for the first time in her long career.

Here's the interesting thing. Not one employee said that Joy had done anything egregious or terminable. In fact, most said that she worked hard, meant well, and knew the blood bank operations (she had been promoted from within). Most also said they didn't like working for her. She wasn't warm or open or fun or happy or any of those things we like to see in our leaders.

But it did not make sense that a socially awkward manager who was no fun would elicit such a disproportionate response and reaction from the team. Something else was happening.

I discovered the catalyst for the team's meltdown when I asked what, if anything, had recently changed. Every one of the team members told me about the new accountability system that had been put in place to improve the safety of the blood supply. Not one member disagreed with the system intellectually—they all wanted to produce safe blood—but they hated how it was being done. Here's how it worked. From the time blood came into the blood bank until the time it exited the department and transfused into a patient, many steps happened to the blood. It was tested, processed, and stored, with checks and balances throughout the process. The bloodbankers had to audit their work, sign off on steps, and document everything. The process was essentially the same as it had always been, but now they had a system for checking for errors at every step. Each morning, Joy would run a report that listed the errors from the day before. Then she would talk to each employee who had made an error, coach him or her, and ask them to sign off that they had been told about the error.

Even though management said that this accountability system was meant to be developmental, team members felt that it was punitive. Even though management said that the signed reports were not going into their personnel files, the employees still felt that they were being "written up." For the first time in their careers, the team members were feeling "not good enough."

Another thing to note is that this accountability system took a lot of the Joy's time to complete. She had to compile the reports, conduct individual counseling sessions, file the signed error sheets (not in the employee file but in some other mystical place), and communicate the results to her manager. This meant that she had even less time to spend with her team, not that she did much of that previously.

You've likely heard of Hertzberg's Hygiene Theory, and it is worth referencing here. Hertzberg studied motivation and found that while things like money and security do not motivate performance, they need to be at an acceptable, or hygiene, level or they will become demotivators. For example, money does not motivate great performance, but if we do not make enough to pay our bills, it becomes a source of stress and reduces our motivation. In the case of our blood bank team, the new accountability system caused a huge hit to the team's sense of safety and security and became a demotivator. Keep in mind that, intellectually, the members of the team thought that holding them accountable for quality work was a good and right thing to do, but the practice broke their hearts and shattered their confidence.

Does this mean that leaders should not try to hold people accountable because it will make them feel bad? No, holding people accountable is critical. But leaders need to realize what accountability systems can do in terms of damaging employee confidence, focus, and perceptions of worth and then counteract these unintended consequences through love.

There I said it. Love. Love! I mean *managerial love*, not the romantic kind, and I will describe exactly what I mean by this a bit later in the book. For now, let me offer that we show managerial love when we take initiative on behalf of someone and when we show our employees that they matter and are important—not just to the company, but to us. Management is a service, and love is where great service comes from.

This case highlighted a perfect storm of circumstances that endangered the team's success, Joy's effectiveness, and the overall success of the accountability system:

- Joy's managing style was on the less caring side of the management spectrum, so the team was craving more love from Joy even before the accountability system was implemented.

- The team itself was highly experienced and emotionally driven.

- The new accountability system offered daily punches in the gut, diverting the non-nurturing manager's time away from potentially more positive communications with her team.

Figure 2.1 offers a visual representation of the blood bank situation.

Figure 2.1. The Bloodbankers' Situation: The Problem

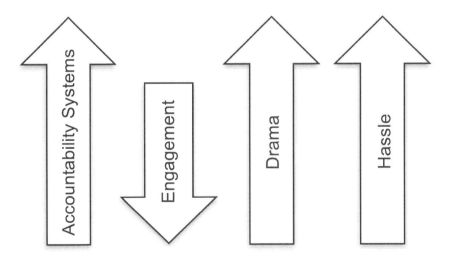

This meant that as the new accountability system was being implemented, the team was also experiencing more work-related hassle and drama. At the same time, efforts to engage employees were going down (and were lower from the start). Let's look at a better scenario as depicted in Figure 2.2.

Figure 2.2. The Bloodbankers' Situation: The Solution

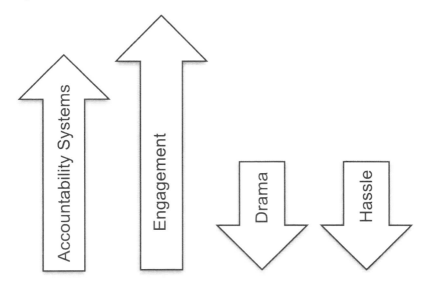

To improve performance velocity, we want to increase well-managed accountability practices and at the same time increase engagement, especially love, all while trying to reduce the hassle and drama that employees experience. This is an ideal situation, but one worth working toward.

Part of my assignment was to recommend whether Joy ought to be fired. What do you think I suggested? Interestingly, Joy had done exactly what she had been told. Her functional director told her to focus whatever time it took to implement the new accountability system. So while she wasn't likely the right fit for the role (or any management role) in the long term, what had happened here was not a terminable event. The functional leader was just as clueless about the tailspin the accountability system could cause for the team, so he did not provide her the coaching she needed in this situation. This is particularly so because Joy had been promoted from within and had very little training in management (and no great role models from which to learn). Sound familiar?

I met with Joy to go over my report and recommendations. I told her that her team issues and the new accountability system were linked. The most important suggestion I had for her was that to make the accountability system work, she needed to double or triple her efforts to show each team member that she cared for them and that they were valued.

Joy said that she didn't have time and didn't know how to do this.

I told her that this was her only choice; showing managerial love was not just a nice thing to do to make the team feel better. The accountability system would not work unless team members were able to put the performance feedback into perspective so that they could learn from it and change their actions to perform better. (This is an important point: The accountability system would not work unless the team could respond to the feedback and improve.) She knew that this was true when I said it because the daily audits were not getting easier and the error rates had not changed for the better. The emotional toll on the team members was acting like a brick wall between them and their ability to look at the performance feedback rationally.

> *The accountability system would not work unless the team could respond to the feedback and improve.*

I spent some time with Joy discussing what "doubling the love" (or tripling, in her case) might look like. One of the greatest opportunities she had was to show them a deep respect for their experience and challenge them to participate in making process improvements. As a previous bloodbanker herself, and one who was respected by the team for her technical expertise, she could use this connection to the team to engage them in a new way. We also discussed ways she could do her daily rounding in ways that seemed more attentive (loving) and less critical.

I also talked with all three of the leaders—the HR leader, the functional leader, and Joy—about some ways to reduce the mental stress being caused by the accountability system. For example, they had communicated to the employees that they were not being "written up" because the signed error sheets did not go in their employee file. This message was a distinction without a difference. Of course they were being written up, and any employee would feel this way. Management either needed to be honest about that or change how it did this.

This blood bank example vividly shows how accountability systems can negatively impact employees and how managers must counterbalance the crud—the mental garbage—that even intellectually sound practices can provoke. (By the way, I really like the word *crud* here because that is generally what it is—the emotional muck of unintended consequences of change.) Every leader uses accountability systems, and most of you are being asked to implement new practices designed to monitor and improve work practices. If you want them to work, it is really important that you think through what might happen and adjust your managerial regimen to ensure that your employees are coachable, open, and productive (versus stressed, defensive, and cornered).

SECRET 2: To make accountability systems work, you may need to double the love. *Counterbalance the crud of change.*

Doubling the love is a very powerful leadership secret, and I hope it resonates with you. It speaks to the importance of being conscious about everything that is going on and the stress caused by seemingly straightforward changes.

Secret 3, our next secret, addresses another possible downside of common accountability practices—in this case, communication.

CHAPTER THREE

Don't Repeat—Resonate

TEDxHouston 2012

I attended the TEDxHouston in 2012 and then blogged about my favorite talk on *Management Craft*. The talk is important to understand for any manager who wants to increase accountability (and even engagement), so I'd like to share the post and explore the connections with you:

Repetition Leads to Brain Pruning: Your Message Might Be a Lullaby, November 8, 2012

I attended TEDxHouston last weekend. It was a nice line up of talks and a great collection of people. One of the talks that I found interesting was offered by Anthony Brandt—a composer, music director, and professor at Rice University. His message was focused on answering the question, "Do Minds Need Art?" His perspective, as you might expect, is that we do.

That's a given; here's what I found fascinating.

Anthony talked about what artistic endeavors do to our brains and how this relates to creativity. He was joined on stage by a string quartet who demonstrated his points through music.

Here's the first point: Repetition "prunes" our brain. I love that word pruning—not that I want to reduce the size of my brain but that it offers a vivid image of what's happening. Anthony used the example of lullabies and why they put us to sleep—they are sweet and droning, the same phrases repeated with little change.

Instead of pruning our brains, art and artistic activities bend, break, or blend. The quartet played snippets of a Beethoven piece showing how he used all these techniques to build drama and interest. As Anthony was talking, I could not help but think about how we communicate in the workplace. Lullaby or Beethoven? What I see is a lot of lullaby and very little Beethoven.

We tell leaders they need to communicate mission/values/goals again and again. And they do, reminding us through mouse pads and video clips. But unless we are going deeper, to the point of bending, breaking, or blending, we are just putting people asleep. To change the culture, we need to persevere/repeat, but we should not do this in ways that prunes our brains. This idea offers leaders an opportunity to combat lackluster vibe and engage our teams in building better futures.

We need to let—encourage actually—employees bend, break, and blend the ideas, and this means that we need to be more flexible. Allow people to create and make the organization's goals and vision their own. Not to the point that the organization goes off course—but in ways that keep it moving forward. Leadership lullabies can be found in everyday workplace practices and messages. Most staff meetings are lullabies.

Wake up your team! Wake yourself up! If you are not creating, you are pruning.

The post captured my immediate reaction and interpretation; I have had a chance to explore this idea further since. I talked with Anthony Brandt, shared my post, and he immediately saw the connections I was making to leadership practices. He shared how neuroscience supports his theory about brain pruning. What does it have to do with accountability? I can think of no managerial system so full of droning lullabies than accountability practices. Our metrics are set, told, and retold to the point they become our goals instead of measures of our goals (resulting in the tail-wagging-the-dog problem so common in organizations). We think that clarifying expectations means using the same corporate speak over and over again. And our performance evaluation conversations become uncomfortable and meaningless meetings to get through (for all involved). The same uninspiring phrases show up repeatedly.

Repetition "prunes" our brains.

True accountability occurs after employees understand what's expected of them in depth and on many layers. What do I mean by "layers"? Most of the managers I have coached or trained start off playing on the surface layer. They communicate goals, have several one-on-ones a year, give some feedback, and then try to do a decent job of giving an accurate evaluation. They post team and department goals on a

> *True accountability occurs after employees understand what's expected of them in depth and on many layers.*

cork board and give updates at staff meetings. That's all surface-level stuff. Are you falling asleep yet? We treat the elements of the accountability system like they are check-the-box requirements, but things are not that simple and here's how I know this. When leaders complain to me that their employees are not meeting their expectations, it is almost never because they are not doing the surface level stuff— the things that you find in SMART (that is, specific, measureable, attainable, realistic, timely . . . and boring) goals. These leaders most often complain about the ways they are getting things done: not the what, the how. Or if it is the what, it is the subtler aspects of it. These are the layers you want your employees to grasp and work toward, and you can't get them there if your messages are pruning their brains and putting them to sleep.

So although I wrote in Secret 1 that accountability systems are limited in what they are designed to do and don't facilitate excellence, they are nonetheless critical and can be very helpful in ensuring that employees are crystal clear about the job they have been asked to do and the contribution you need them to make to the organization. To ensure that your time is well spent, you will want your accountability conversations to resonate with people. To resonate means to build in meaning, reflection about, and connection to the information. The deeper you go in terms of layers of communication, the more your team members will understand the finer points of how you are defining expectations and their performance. It's these finer points that tend to either trip up people or enable them to succeed.

SECRET 3: Droning accountability measures and goals into people's heads puts them to sleep. *Don't repeat; resonate.*

You have seen employees roll their eyes when leaders preach to them. You may have experienced what it is like to speak to a group who just sit and stare at you. It's very weird, and it sucks to be on the receiving end of such dismissiveness. Realize, however, that these nonverbal expressions are clues that your words are putting them to sleep. Passing out Klondike ice cream bars would be a better use of your time. Or, you could say something that makes an impact—yes, that's the ticket.

The next secret, **Secret 4**, builds on the idea that what we do each day matters a lot.

CHAPTER FOUR

Persevere

No Surprises Denny

I worked with a leader at a large high-tech manufacturer who had accountability grit. His name was Denny and if you worked for him, you knew where you stood and whether you needed to make any performance adjustments. Denny was religious about having one-on-ones with all his employees, during which he discussed goals, behaviors, and the individual's development plan. I was an internal organization development (OD) consultant but worked closely with both operations and HR. Denny had a reputation as being someone who would take care of performance issues right when they emerged, and he was firm and fair. He was a pretty serious guy when there was something that needed his attention but always gave his teams personalized attention to check in and to resolve their issues.

Come performance evaluation time, employees already had a good idea of how their performance stacked up against what was expected. Denny made sure that there were never any surprises (oh, how I wish we all would follow Denny's lead on this!) and that the time spent during the evaluation was focused on summarizing the performance rating and focusing on future goals and development planning. I was struck by the lack of angst that Denny and his employees felt during evaluation time compared to others.

Denny was a consistent and effective communicator with peers and his boss too. He made sure that everyone was aware of short-term and long-term goals, his teams' action plans, and how issues were being resolved. He made sure there were no surprises on his shift, and this made his employees and others feel a sense of comfort and trust.

I realize that I have made Denny's leadership routines seem rather simple here—they were anything but that. He worked hard to ensure that everyone knew what he expected and how they stood, and he spent a lot of his time on his shift talking with employees—and he communicated in ways that got deeper than the surface and that resonated (see previous secret). It was an effective regimen that he honed (without droning) over years of practice.

> **Denny made sure there were never any surprises.**

No Grit for Sally

For part of my career, I served as the head of HR for a travel company, and Denny could have taught its leadership team a thing or two. I remember meeting with the executive team for one of our divisions to help them conduct their talent review, a process by which the senior team assesses the performance and potential of their employees and whether they might be a possible successor for a broader role. Everything was going fine until we began discussing one particular product manager. I am going to call her Sally.

The executive team of about eight members was united in its assessment of Sally. Members of the team said she was not meeting expectations and had little potential to grow beyond her role. Here's roughly how the conversation went from there:

> *Me:* How long has she not been meeting your expectations?
>
> *Team:* For years. She is highly talented on the technical side but is divisive and a poor team player. We have had people quit because of her.
>
> *Me:* So why does she still work here?
>
> *Team:* She knows a lot about her itineraries and knows all the suppliers. It would be hard to replace her technical skillset.
>
> *Me:* Let me ask you something. If I were to look up her last three performance evaluations, would I see this addressed?

Team: Yes. Well, somewhat. We have told her that she needs to be a better team player.

Me: And did that work?

Team: No.

Me: And has anything bad happened to her as a result?

Team: No.

Me: OK, then she is meeting your expectations.

Team: No, she is not.

Me: Yes, she is. Here's the thing. Expectations exist "out there" and are something you reinforce every day with each action and conversation. Telling Sally that she needs to be a better team member during her performance evaluation (where you rate her well overall and give her a raise) and then ignoring her unwillingness to address this developmental need is not enough. In fact, your actions have communicated to your entire team, not just Sally, that you do not expect good team skills and that bullying, badgering, and divisiveness are acceptable behaviors.

Team: But we do expect employees to be great team members.

Me: No, you don't. Your actions say otherwise.

Finally, the light bulbs started going on in their heads, one by one. Performance expectations are created by hundreds of leadership actions. Which expectations are you willing to share, measure, reinforce, and hold others accountable for?

I have seen this same scenario play out many times. Leaders ask me for advice about how to improve XYZ performance, and we discover that the desired behaviors are not being consistently reinforced or discussed deeply enough. I understand that it is no fun to crack the whip and harp on people about what they need to do (remember the previous secret?). I understand that as a busy leader, holding people accountable takes a lot of time. But because accountability is a compliance-driven system, consistency and regularity are the keys to its success. Your true

> *Expectations are something you reinforce every day with each action and conversation.*

expectations are those that you reinforce by your actions, not just those idealized intentions you communicate, no matter how well or how often.

Have you ever worked for a place that seemed to ruin great talent? Imagine you have a low-productivity team and you hire a hotshot performer that you think will be a great influence on others. After a few months, the new guy is performing no better than anyone else! What happened? The new guy figured out that your expectations of your team are really quite pitiful, and so he lowered his effort to meet them! It happens a lot.

In Section II we will explore specific ways to build rock-solid accountability practices, but for now, keep in mind that the greatest indicator of whether you will have highly accountable teams is your perseverance.

SECRET 4: The secret to accountability is grit. *Persevere.*

This secret might make you feel dumped on, but that is not my intent. I realize that if you are already feeling like you can't get everything done, suggesting that you need to do more to persevere might seem like a slap in the face. But hang on and don't lose faith. We will address this challenge in Section II.

Secret 5 begins our exploration of engagement.

CHAPTER FIVE

Take Initiative on Behalf of Someone Else

From Learned Helplessness to Loved

This is a sweet love story. When I was the head of HR for a travel company, we struggled with a very-low-performing team. Team members behaved in ways that made it seem as if they hated their work and could not wait to leave each day. When employees from other departments asked for their help or partnership, they seemed angry and put out.

We knew that the manager was part of the problem, but we weren't sure how much. I am going to call this manager Bob. Like his team, Bob seemed unengaged and unhappy. He had very low expectations of his team—which meant that from an accountability standpoint, most were meeting his expectations. But in addition to low expectations, Bob did not give his people the care and attention they needed. They seemed sapped of their interest (personally, I find apathy harder to deal with than anger, don't you?). The team seemed like a classic case of learned helplessness—a condition that occurs when individuals fail to help themselves or advocate on their own behalf because they perceive they have no control or can have no impact. Bob had not been listening to or caring for his team members for so long that they stopped assuming anyone cared. I tried coaching Bob, but he was not interested in changing. We terminated Bob.

Several senior leaders partnered to recruit and hire Bob's replacement. We narrowed the search to two top candidates. The first had more experience leading this type of function; he was very sharp and savvy. The second candidate was a fire hose of energy, passion, and raw talent; he was scrappy but wicked smart. Most of the folks on the selection team preferred the more experienced candidate, and, indeed, he was the safest choice. But there was something about the second guy that told me he would try harder to turn this team around. After successfully making my case, we hired the human fire hose. I will call him Tim.

Tim immediately made his new team members uneasy. They were clear that this was a new day and that things would change. They were fearful, but they also had not felt so alive in years. Tim did hundreds of things to facilitate a turnaround, and all but a couple of the team members became high-performing employees. He and I met often and talked about the practices that would create a more accountable and engaging work environment. Tim knew that to change the culture he needed to give this team a high level of positive attention every day. And that is what he did.

> **The work environment must be enriching enough that employees choose to engage in it. Think magnet.**

As we touched on earlier, engagement is a *pull* system—the work environment must be enriching enough that employees *choose* to engage in it. *Think magnet.* (Accountability, by contrast, is more like a corral.) While engagement is a choice and driven by our employees, what we do as leaders makes a tremendous difference. In particular, the ways we take the initiative to make things better (or don't) have a huge impact on engagement.

I call this type of initiative taking *managerial love* (I told you it would be a love story!). I realize that this term might not be comfortable for some people to use, but please get over any hang-ups you have about it. It's the perfect phrase! *Managerial love is taking initiative on behalf of someone else.* I love that definition, don't you? It makes sense and mirrors what we experience with our loved ones. When our spouse or child does something for us that we did not expect—like doing the dishes without being asked because we have a headache—we feel loved. We consider this proactive and giving act to be the demonstration of their love. My husband, Bill, is not a sappy romantic, but I am blown away every day by the ways that he shows care and consideration for me. I might never get a surprise chocolate diamond ring from him (hint), but he will be the first to completely re-stock our kitchen and produce a whole new set of dinner items every time I latch onto a new fad diet—which occurs about weekly. He does this without apparent frustration at my flakiness. It's a genuine expression of love—and much cheaper than the diamond.

The same is true in the workplace. "But wait a minute, Lisa," you might be wondering, "are you assuming I actually love my employees?" In a way, yes I am. When we accept a leadership role, we adopt one or more teams of people. We accept responsibility for our employees, and we know that we will have a big impact on their lives, not just their work (you do know this, right?). Leading people is a service-oriented, care-taking role, and part of that role is an assumption that you will show care and act on behalf of your employees. That, my friends, is love.

Back to Tim's story. To turn around the low-performing team, Tim improved the accountability system, which helped a lot. But the things he did that made the biggest positive difference fell into the category of managerial love. Tim took an active interest in each team member and tried to connect with each person for a few moments each day. He listened more than talked, although he also showed love by including them in conversations about the department's future. He showed the team, through his words and actions and even his smile, that he assumed the team could succeed and that each team member had important talents. He took the initiative to learn the strengths of his employees and made several role changes that enabled them to contribute more fully. He mentored a couple of folks who were struggling with stress due to change and was patient where and when he could be. Tim was fun and infused a much-needed energy into the department. He encouraged team members to help spruce up the office, adding colors and textures. And he challenged the team in nonthreatening ways. They slowly reengaged in the work. Tim knew that there was a reason they chose their jobs in the first place; he just needed to help reinvigorate their intrinsic motivation. All of this is love—taking the initiative on behalf of someone else. It's a beautiful thing, and we know when we are receiving it and we are warmed by it.

Some leaders are naturally more comfortable giving managerial love, but I believe that we all can learn to be great. When we were interviewing Tim, I knew that he would put more effort into saving this team. His past successes prepared him for this. The other candidate was very qualified on the technical aspects of running the function, but I did not see a lot of managerial love in the examples he shared about his previous job accomplishments. Could he have learned how to be a more loving leader? I have no doubt that he could, but we needed someone who would be able to nurture and care for this broken team from day one.

SECRET 5: The secret to engagement is managerial love. *Take initiative on behalf of someone else.*

How explicitly are you giving managerial love? I realize that the juxtaposition of the words *explicit* and *love* will make my HR friends squirm, but I don't care because they are the right words here. If you want high employee engagement, the greatest determining factor will be your level of proactivity in providing managerial love. I am convinced of this and have seen it play out hundreds of times.

In Section II, we will get into the nitty-gritty of what managerial love looks like in action. For now, let's explore **Secret 6**, which represents what happens when our employees don't get enough managerial love.

CHAPTER SIX

Request Humbly

Zeva, the VP of HR

I worked for a leader who knew Secret 6 well. I will call her Zeva. You know how some people can instantly say the right things and make you want to move mountains? Zeva was that type of leader—but not because she was a salesperson or because she knew how to use positive reinforcement to praise people. Her impact came from the fact that you knew that she was thankful for the effort you were putting into the work. More than anyone I have ever worked for, Zeva could tell when employees were highly engaged in their work. She distinguished full engagement and received it like a pleasant surprise. "Surprise" is not the right word, because she certainly knew we were capable, but she never gave us the sense that she took our extra efforts for granted.

I can remember talking with Zeva about a program I had launched that had gone quite well. It was a training session for a group of finicky senior executives. She told me that the secret sauce, what made it work, was that I was fully present with them in the conversation, not facilitating outside of it. She said that my deep listening enabled me to connect, understand, and respond in ways that changed the whole vibe of the day. A couple of the participants challenged the concepts I was sharing, but through respectful discussion they came around and ended up making points that helped everyone learn. The session was well designed and implemented, but she said that the best part was that I played big during the program and put every ounce of my energy into being a catalyst for their learning. She knew what it took to do that, she saw that I showed up ready to rock and roll, and she made sure that I knew she was grateful. And even though this occurred many years ago, I remember the conversation like it was yesterday because of the way she made me feel.

There is a difference between doing an OK job and giving it your all. Some leaders, organizations, and teams make us want to do our very best. Others inspire only "meets expectations" work.

I have to vent here. I find that many of my HR colleagues are totally clueless about why we all hate being told we "meet expectations" on our performance evaluation. They rationalize that this rating is actually really good because we have high expectations and when you meet these expectations it means that you are doing great work. And they say that we should be proud and happy to get a "meets expectations" rating and that we have to work very hard to achieve this level of performance. *Bravo, I'm meeting expectations*! This is just bunk, and I am laughing as I am writing this because I can recall training sessions where smart, well-meaning HR leaders stood in front of groups and said these silly things. First of all, I have worked for several *Fortune* 50 organizations known for their evaluation systems as well as many other successful companies, and in none of them was it very hard to get a "meets expectations" rating. Why? Because, for the most part, we (leaders) are too chicken to give someone anything less than this.

But I digress. Back to the point that we don't actually like being told we meet expectations. Why is this important to acknowledge and, perhaps more important, why is this related to this secret? You know in your heart that no one wants to be told they are meeting expectations. OK, perhaps 1 percent of your employees, who were previously put on a performance improvement

> *Engagement is not a job description item. It is a gift and a precious one at that.*

plan, want to be told they are meeting expectations. The other 99 percent want to be told they are amazing. And although most everyone is an average performer (that's why they call it average), we know that sometimes it takes every ounce of our being to get things done. As performers, we want to feel like our leaders know and appreciate when we give it our all. As leaders, we should recognize that engagement is not a job description item. It is a gift and a precious one at that. Zeva knew this and she was able to ask for my best with a grace that enabled the conversation to transcend the world of expectations. Ari, on the other hand, was not as grateful a boss.

Ari, the Crappy Boss

There is nothing more agonizing than coaching a talented, hardworking, well-intended professional who works for a crappy boss. When he or she asks me for advice on what to do, what do you think I say? It depends on the circumstances, but the answers generally cluster around the following options:

- Don't let your boss's faults get in your way or get you down. Just do good work and make an impact wherever you can. Get satisfaction from this.

- Bail. Life is too short.

- Your manager is a cancer; you need to share your experiences with the next level up.

All of these responses are unsatisfactory on some level. As leaders, we should never put our employees in the position of having to resort to one of these responses.

I knew a leader who I will call Ari. Ari led a team of fifteen HR professionals. His team was in a perpetual state of forming or adjusting team dynamics with new people. Open jobs were the norm, and there were always new people because so many team members left or asked for transfers. Ironically, because several members got their transfer requests approved, Ari considered himself a talent builder for the entire organization. Talk about poor self-awareness! What did Ari do that was so unappealing? He talked of empowerment but held all the plum projects for himself. Did he have time to complete all these projects? No, which meant that he was too busy and therefore not available for his team. He sucked the life and air out of meetings and wasn't at all open to new ideas or suggestions. His team didn't feel supported or cared for. Ari's team was structured so that their workloads were enormous and filled with uninspiring tasks, which in turn resulted in high burnout rates. Even Ari didn't seem engaged or happy. Bleh!

Ari talked to his team about wanting them to engage more fully. Indeed, their department goals were challenging and needed everyone's best efforts to succeed. But would you pour your heart and soul into your work if you had a manager like Ari? Perhaps for a while, but eventually even the most giving, dedicated employees would lose their spark for the work.

We have all known, and maybe worked for, crappy bosses. This is nothing new and certainly not a secret. The reason I think it is important to discuss here is that I have known many leaders who have not made the connection between their actions and their employees' engagement. Engagement is a pull system, and so we need to behave in ways that create pull. Bad leaders, or even mediocre leaders with too many annoying practices, do not deserve to expect engagement. It is even more aggravating to work for a crappy boss who "expects" high levels of engagement. Well guess what, crappy boss, you can't expect engagement because engagement is a gift.

Now think of your own management approach. Would you say that you are more like Zeva or Ari? Consider the impact you are having on

> *You can only expect your employees to be as engaged as you appear to be.*

your team right now. Are you working for them in ways that inspire them to do their best for you? Most leaders are so caught up in the rat race, or mice's maze, or daily fire fights (or pick your own metaphor for workload overwhelm) that they fail to bring life to their workplace (and may inadvertently cause stress and drain). As we explored in the previous secret, engagement requires some explicit effort—transmitting a feeling of interest, care, or passion for the work. In other words, your employees need to experience a boss who is a pleasure to work with and who is highly engaged. You can only expect your employees to be as engaged as you appear to be. This is one of those times when being a role model is not just a nice thing to do; it is the price of admission.

And beyond being a great role model, are you grateful for the extra efforts your team members give you? Do they know that you know what it takes to make things happen and that you appreciate it all? Reread my recollections about how Zeva acknowledged my work and think about the ways you can ensure that your team members know that you understand this secret.

SECRET 6: Engagement is a gift you might not have earned. *Request humbly.*

Many bosses, unfortunately, are not regular sources of gratitude, energy, or inspiration. The good news is that there are things we can do to improve, and we will explore them in detail in Section II.

The next secret, **Secret 7**, is a doozy—and one that might make you think differently about how to manage your best performers.

CHAPTER SEVEN

Challenge Even Your Best

Barry, the Incredible

Barry was a high-performing senior leader for major manufacturing company. He was high energy, fun to work with, and open to new approaches. I really enjoyed working with him when I served as an internal OD consultant in his organization. Barry was my largest client, and we had a very productive partnership. He stayed current in his field, mentored others, and had a great reputation for delivering excellent results. He engaged his staff in meaningful conversations and took initiative to create a challenging team environment. His function outperformed others, and people wanted to join his team. Barry was very good at building an engaging workplace, and he had the grit to ensure high accountability.

The division president, who made sure Barry knew how important he was to the company, had no idea that he was about to lose him.

I can remember the three-hour car ride I made with Barry on the way to a meeting at our company's headquarters. Our conversation started with typical work-related stuff but then turned to a deep discussion about job satisfaction. As it turned out, Barry was bored, burned out, and felt unengaged. He wanted something more; something that might get his heart and mind racing again. Even though he was the highest performing leader in our division, he ached for something harder so that he could enjoy his work and grow as a leader.

Barry left the company about six months later. He was recruited to lead a complex start-up. He told me that he looked forward to having a job that would require he do his best and then some. He left because he wanted work that enlivened his intrinsic motivations for solving tough problems, fostering innovation, and delivering uncommon results.

Have you ever felt like Barry? I remember the day I decided to start looking for a new job while I was still at Black & Decker. I had been there four years, the first two of which were among the best of my entire career. I was asked to do things I had never done before, and the stakes were high. I loved it! I was promoted to the corporate headquarters and enjoyed the first year of that job too (although it was not as challenging, ironically, and not as fun for me). I started getting bored two years into my promotion and I can remember meeting with my VP of HR to discuss a few ideas I had for the coming year. What he said convinced me that it was time to move on. He said something like, "slow down, things are great, let's just take it easy, and maintain what we are doing."

Have you ever left a perfectly good job and company to take a risk on a new job and company because you needed something more? I think it happens more than we realize. I have had the pleasure of working with many extraordinary professionals and have noticed that far too many are simultaneously

Your best performers might be striving—but then again they might just be coasting.

high performing and unengaged. Seems odd that these two conditions would coexist, but let's think through this a bit more. The definition of what it means to be engaged is that we pour our hearts and minds into something, do our best work, strive, and are intrinsically motivated. This looks different for each person. Your best performers might be striving—but then again, they might just be coasting.

The HiPots

When conducting a talent review, leaders assess the performance and potential of all or part of their employee population to determine their most promotable employees and to evaluate overall bench strength. We often call the employees who are rated high in performance and potential, "HiPots." Several years ago, I was asked to work with a group of HiPots. My assignment was to help them create effective development plans and to coach them throughout the year.

This was a great project and I enjoyed working with these top performers. They were interested, curious, and super smart. But most were also fairly disengaged overall. Disengaged? How could this be?

If you ask leaders which employees get most of their attention, many will admit that their low performers suck up the greatest amount of time. Then the folks in the middle. And the top performers are usually pretty independent, because they do not need the leader's attention. This makes some sense because, as a busy leader, you need to apply energy where it is most needed.

> *As leaders we routinely under-inspire and under-challenge our top talent.*

It is also common that we do not challenge our best performers because we feel they are already doing their part, plus some. This, too, makes sense if you are managing based on an expectation of roughly equal contributions from each team member.

Quite simply, many of the HiPots I was coaching seemed bored and uninspired. Even though they were already contributing more than other team members, they were just going through the motions. It's a bit like telling a champion race horse: "Don't worry about running today."

I believe that as leaders we routinely under-inspire and under-challenge our top talent. When I think back to all of my bosses and jobs, only one truly motivated me to try my best. Only one. What a shame and a waste! It is also a common cause of turnover of high potentials because they reason that even if the new job isn't more challenging, at least the newness of the environment and circumstances will be fun to figure out.

What might be possible if you fully challenged and inspired your best performers? And when was the last time you invested some managerial love in the direction of your best performers? Not just to tell them they're great but to ignite their passion to contribute on a big scale? This is one of those ideas that seems a bit counterintuitive, but it is important that we require more from our top performers.

It has been said that if you are the smartest person in the room, you are in the wrong room. This is so true and a common reason that our best and brightest leave our teams and organizations. Are you ensuring that your most talented team members get to work—even if only on a special project—with people who will bring out their best? People they look up to and admire? This idea has huge implications for leaders who want to fully engage their best contributors.

SECRET 7: Your most talented, highest performing employees might also be your least engaged. *Challenge even your best.*

This is sobering, right? I hope this secret has you thinking about your top performers and how you might challenge and inspire them even more than you are today. Engagement takes effort, but I know that all leaders can be extraordinarily engaging. I know it!

The next secret, **Secret 8**, reveals your secret weapon in engaging others.

CHAPTER EIGHT

Be Your Brand of Amazing

Highly Talented, Deeply Flawed

What if I told you that one of your most powerful tools to increase engagement is something that should come quite naturally to you? What is this powerful tool? It's your special something.

When I first met David, a chief operating officer for a service organization, I was not impressed. He seemed a bit clueless in terms of how people operate, and I thought his tendency to think linearly was a weakness. And yet David had a knack for engaging his team and getting them excited about overcoming their challenges. Did he do this through charm? No way. Did he do this through bribery with cupcakes? No. (Don't laugh, this is one of the most common tactics I see unenlightened leaders attempt.) Did he do this through salesmanship? Hardly. David's secret weapon was engineering. Now keep in mind, his teams were not engineers, nor did they do engineering work. But David thought like an engineer, and so he leveraged this strength to engage his team.

He asked great questions, listened well, considered all information, didn't jump to conclusions, and involved people in meaty discussions. His team of mostly marketing and sales types loved the approach and felt well cared for because David was genuine and did not try to be someone he was not.

This basic example highlights an important ingredient of this secret. Actually, it is not basic at all—it is a compelling truth. Your special essence, your uniqueness, what's most interesting about you holds your greatest potential to engage people. Our team members will be most inspired when we are authentic and passionate about the work—in our own way. They will get to know what our brand of managerial love looks like and be very thankful to receive it. Do you know what your secret weapon—

Your special essence, your uniqueness, what's most interesting about you holds your greatest potential to engage people.

or superpower, if you prefer—is? (Knowing what it's not is also very important.) If you are not sure, ask a few people who know you well to help you figure it out.

When I make presentations or facilitate leadership training sessions, I notice the ideas and phrases that resonate with participants. One such idea is that we are all highly talented and highly flawed. It is a simple idea and nothing that we don't already know. The reason it resonates is that many of us have not internalized what this really means in terms of how we impact others.

Our school systems, performance evaluations, and 360-degree assessments all reinforce the notion that we should be strong performers in every area. I suppose a few of you are, but most of us are lopsided performers. We do some things better than most people, and we stink at other things.

Because management is a social act (and therefore very visible), everyone knows our strengths and our weaknesses. You might see this reality as rather frightening, but I invite you to see it as freeing and comforting. If our strengths and weaknesses are known, then there is no downside to being open about them, right? We don't lose credibility by acknowledging and owning our weaknesses. I am not saying that you should not care about the things you do poorly (for example, being a micromanager, which is very bad and drives people away). But I am saying that if you want to create a highly engaging workplace, you must use your strengths and skills.

For example, as an OD and training professional, facilitation is the essence of my nature (heck, I even try to facilitate discussions with my dogs, which never works). You can bet that I rely on a lot of facilitation-type activities to engage my team members. I also make numerous connections for people so they can get unstuck. It's what I know, and it works well to pull people in and get them engaged.

If you are like more David, however, and think like an engineer, then apply that skill set to challenge your team members. If you are a natural-born salesperson, get to know your employees' interests and the features and benefits of the workplace that will provide the most value. I once worked for an Austrian chef who saw everything as a potential work of art. It was a blast, and he challenged me to see the elegance in everyday

Use what you have; it's significant!

work processes and to guard against diminishing the beauty of how we work. One of my key internal clients was a man who was very well read. He exposed me to ideas, models, and metaphors that came from novels and memoirs because that is what he knew best. I loved all these approaches and grew as a professional because my leaders shared their unique strengths with me.

SECRET 8: You have a secret weapon you can use to engage others. *Be your brand of amazing.*

Use what you have; it's significant! I am not suggesting that you force your preferences onto your employees or that you limit your approaches to those with which you are comfortable. Remember, engagement is a pull system; push won't work. But the good news is that there are many ways to be great at this; discover how to leverage your greatness.

The next secret, **Secret 9**, addresses a common error that destroys engagement and reveals a mindset shift that can make the error disappear.

CHAPTER NINE

Ask for the Real Stuff

Great Scores, Undeserved

As a consultant, I created, administered, and shared results for many employee surveys. I will never forget one leadership team I worked with, because they received amazingly high employee engagement survey scores that they had not earned. And the kicker is that their situation is not all that unique. Let me explain.

The employee engagement survey project started off fine. The leadership team wanted feedback about employee engagement. It would then launch action plans and offer management training based on the areas of most need. Managers would be held accountable to improve their scores.

Months prior to the survey launch, the leadership team started talking to the employees about the survey and the types of things they would be asked to rate. The team asked employees for input on ways it could improve engagement. The leaders did not get a lot of ideas from employees, but they kept asking and thanked employees who shared suggestions.

As the two-week survey period began, they held daily raffles for people who completed the survey (things like iPads) and communicated that they had a goal of 75 percent participation. Every day, they sent email updates to managers listing every department's response rates and encouraged them to do whatever they could to ensure at least 75 percent participation.

The survey scores that came back were very good. On a five-point scale, most items were above 4.5 on average. The leadership team believed that their scores indicated they were doing things right.

I bet some of you are thinking, "What's the problem, Lisa? This seems about right." Overall, you are correct that the leadership team approached the survey the way many organizations do and interpreted the results the way most organizations would. I did not see it that way, however. Here are the two key issues I perceived:

1. *They were totally focused on the survey, not employee engagement.* Sure, the survey was designed to measure employee engagement, but when all you talk about is the survey, the survey questions, the survey timeline, and the survey participation, you communicate to your employees that the survey scores are what you are most interested in. This tail-wagging-the-dog problem ends up reinforcing the tool instead of what the tool is designed to measure. I once consulted on a project for a *Fortune* 50 organization that spent millions and millions of dollars on their employee survey and suffered from this skewed focus. Do I think that the leaders were honestly interested in the feedback? Somewhat, yes, but they had allowed themselves to become completely focused on the process, outcomes, and measures of the survey and had lost the true intent and meaning that drove the leaders to ask for feedback in the first place.

2. *They applied incentives and goals (extrinsic) to the process and thereby destroyed the accuracy of the information.* When employees are coached on the questions ahead of time, when employees are given rewards to complete the survey, when managers are held to participation numbers, and when managers are incentivized on improving their results year-over-year, we create artificial motivations for completing surveys and providing high scores. I know of a few leaders who gave their employees an incentive goal that paid out if they got good employee survey scores. This

makes no sense at all and is, in fact, ridiculous. Here's the kicker—these leaders honestly thought that what they were doing was OK and that their survey results were valid.

We—leaders in the corporate world—do many inadvertently dumb things that produce the opposite of our intentions. The ways we use employee surveys often makes me want to scream, especially when what we do reveals that what we say is fake. Does this sound familiar?

> We care about your feedback and will use it to improve the workplace. We invite you to be candid and open and to share your experiences. We want to earn a "5," and we'd like you to tell us what we can do to get a "5" rating on the next survey.

I know you have all heard this—the strive-for-five campaigns. What gets me a little riled up is that I have known leaders who actually think this is a good and OK thing. Leaders who use versions of the strive-for-five method must realize that their words are fake. But it's not just that they are fake—they cause damage to the workplace that will be tough to repair (because a breach of trust is one of the most difficult organizational issues to overcome). When we strive for five we are saying, "I don't actually care about your feedback. I have to meet my goal and that's what I care about." This is not the message we want to send, and I think we should challenge each other to focus on what's really important—even if your boss, or your boss's boss, is measuring you on the numbers.

Most survey scores do not represent reality.

Most of the survey scores I have seen (and I have seen a lot) do not represent reality. The workplace is full of variability, and each organization (and manager) does some things very well and others not well at all.

If you are doing something that is not working for your employees, you truly want to know this, right? So here is my question to you: What could you do that would make giving you that tough-to-hear feedback a very positive experience? If you genuinely want to know the practices that are making your employees want to engage and those that are shutting them down, you want sharing the tough truth to feel like eating a banana split. With energy, smiles, and thank yous at the end.

As a manager, you know how hard it is to share with employees that something they are doing is not working and could get in the way of their careers. You outline your points, talk to HR, plan the meeting, wring your hands, and then nervously deliver the message. Now, imagine what it must be like for your employees to tell you (or the organization) what's not working and how it might get in the way of their engagement and retention. And "What if you could turn that situation around and make giving honest feedback, even the tough stuff, a positive and comfortable experience for everyone involved?" Interested?

SECRET 9: Surveys matter when you love lower scores more than higher ones. *Ask for the real stuff and let it affect how you lead.*

Do you think this shift is possible? I do, but I know it might be tough because how we approach surveys is often common across the organization. We will explore several paths forward in Section II.

This next secret, **Secret 10**, totally blew my mind when I uncovered it. Hold on to your hats!

CHAPTER TEN

Do What Matters

The Western Hospital Group

A group of six hospitals I worked with several years ago was experiencing a crisis with middle manager roles. Many of the managers felt burned out, many were not meeting performance expectations, and few internal candidates applied for promotions to middle management. The hospital system asked me to look into what was going on and make recommendations. Before I started meeting with a sampling of their 600 middle managers, I asked the executive team to tell me about their culture and core values. Among other things, several mentioned that they valued time and inclusion (plus the predictable things like quality care, compassion, and such.). I interviewed and shadowed dozens of leaders and held several focus group discussions. I noticed that the theme of "time" kept coming up. Time was a big deal here for this health system but not in the way the executives might have guessed. After analyzing the information and creating a "day in the life" profile of the average middle manager, I presented my report to the executive team.

My first statement caused an immediate negative reaction. It went something like this:

> *Me*: You told me that you value time, but I see no evidence of this. In fact, you behave as if time is worthless.
>
> *Executive Team:* We do value time. It is precious. What you are saying is incorrect.

> *Me:* Based on how you work and the choices you and your
> managers make about time, I can only conclude that you believe
> time is a commodity and not a value.

I could see that I had made the executive team angry, and I imagined they were regretting hiring me for this project. But I pressed on and eventually made my point in a way they could hear. Several facts led me to the conclusion that they did not value time:

- Middle managers spent an average of 35 hours each week in meetings, over half of which they felt were ineffective.

- Middle managers served on an average of six committees, each requiring travel for meetings.

- Most middle managers could not keep up with their incoming emails. They tended to include everybody on everything and did a lot of "reply all," to CYA (cover their arses). Most of the nurse managers, the job title of most of the middle managers, tried to get caught up on emails on Sundays. They also suffered from a bad reputation as being unresponsive because they often did not answer emails for several days or weeks.

- They valued inclusion at the expense of time. Everyone was included in everything, and if you were left off a meeting notice, it was perceived as a bad thing. It was also expected that if someone added you to a meeting invite, and you had the time open, you would accept, even if your participation was not a good use of your time.

- Support functions—like HR and finance—routinely asked middle managers to do things that took a lot of time but didn't seem to make a positive difference. The processes they had to use for hiring, evaluations, and purchasing were complex and inefficient.

There were many other things on the list, but I think you get the idea. Valuing time means that you make conscious and wise decisions about how you spend it. This organization did not do this. Is it unique? No! I have seen the same issues playing out in many of the organizations with which I have worked. This problem is not new or uncommon, but it is rare that leaders think about the consequences of treating time as a cheap commodity.

You might be wondering: "Lisa, you have lost me, why are you mentioning this here? Why is this a secret and how does it fit with the others?" A key theme we have been exploring in Secrets 1–9 is that performance velocity, which is fueled through high accountability and engagement, takes both grit and love. If you have a lot of change going on (and who

> *Time is our currency for getting things done.*

doesn't?), you might need to implement new accountability systems and double the love. And if you agree with my definition of managerial love as taking initiative on behalf of someone else, then by this point in the book you might be worried that you don't have time to lead well.

I want you to feel excited and optimistic about using these secrets, not stressed out. If you are a busy leader…. well, you are all busy… if you are a leader who struggles to get the most important things done, this secret might be your most important to explore further.

I learned the lesson of this secret about ten years ago and I feel lucky that I did. I was a type-A, career-oriented professional who let the craziness of mile-long to-do lists and "death by meeting" (hat tip to Patrick Lencioni and his brilliantly titled book by the same name) take over my life. In other words, I was normal. And then I started observing leaders who had better ways to manage their time, and I changed completely how I use mine. Since leadership is a social act, time is our currency for getting things done. It is more precious than money or chocolate diamonds.

I will share lots of examples about this in Section II, but for now I want you to believe that you can value time and have that value show up in your actions.

SECRET 10: Most managers think time is precious but behave like it is worthless. *Do what matters.*

Time is all you have, and all that you can control and shape. Previous secrets have established that accountability requires grit and that engagement requires a proactive effort to provide managerial love. These things take time and attention, and the decisions you make each day about how to spend your time are among your most important.

This idea of shaping our days to produce the best results leads us to our final secret, **Secret 11**.

CHAPTER ELEVEN

Be Intentional and Create the World You Seek

Robert

I was coaching a smart, hard-working professional who struggled with feelings of being overwhelmed and with poor results orientation. I will call her Janice. It's not that she did not want to get things done; she felt like she could never get out from under her to-do list. She needed to move from being an entirely reactive leader to a more proactive one.

Janice set me off with a whine about how she did not have time for something that was reportedly very important to her (a four-hour training session that she really needed but that she had cancelled at the last minute—twice). I shared with Janice a story about Robert to illustrate a point about the difference between choice and design. I don't like to draw comparisons between people, but it seemed apropos to point out that there are many leaders with equally or more challenging jobs who have a greater command of their schedules. And honestly, I felt Janice needed a proverbial two-by-four upside her head!

Robert was a great role model in the areas that Janice struggled. He oversaw four major operating groups within the organization and yet was one of the most proactive and responsive leaders with which I worked. If you asked ten of Robert's colleagues about his reputation, they would have likely said that he

- is always on time and does not have to reschedule meetings very often

- does what he says he will

- mentors and coaches more than most leaders

- spends time teaching leadership courses

- always has a plan

- is religious about holding regular one-on-ones with employees

- takes the initiative to spend time with direct reports every day

- is interested in new approaches and loves to participate in future-oriented discussions

- does many things to reinforce accountability and foster engagement

- is a responsive communicator—including fast response to emails

And yet, Robert has a huge job and has as much or more going on as leaders who seem more like Janice—always running behind. How does Robert do it? The answer is that Robert uses effective design principles. That's right, design. He is the architect of his leadership realm, and he has set it up to produce particular outcomes. Remember my previous stories about Denny (Secret 4) and Tim (Secret 5)? They were great designers, too.

What Do I Mean by Design?

When civil engineers design a planned community, they consider things such as how people move and congregate, traffic patterns, what kind of people the community will attract, the type of housing these people will prefer, efficient utility structures, recreational facilities, shopping, safety, and hundreds of other things. All the elements of the design come together to make the community work.

Design is everywhere and relates to all aspects of our lives, including and especially our work. In his book, *A Whole New Mind*, Dan Pink described design as "utility enhanced by significance." I like this definition because it speaks to the "why" of design. We create or change a design to produce a particular impact. And that's why the importance of design is reserved for our final secret. Everything we have been talking about in Secrets 1–10 has focused on seeing a higher possibility for how you can cultivate accountability and engagement in ways that work for you and your employees. To be the type of leader who makes an extraordinary impact, you are going to need to use design.

Performance velocity occurs when our teams perform well—with speed (movement, progress) and direction (on path, creative, focused, working on what most matters). The workplace is the context within which you will create favorable conditions for great results. As a leader, you engineer your workplace communities. You consider, plan,

Design is everywhere and relates to all aspects of our lives, including and especially our work.

create, and re-create many interconnected pieces such as how people will work and come together, vehicles for communication, performance systems, cultural elements, support processes, relationships, skills development, and hundreds of other things.

Design is a decision we make about the future. What will something look like? How will staff meetings be conducted? How will I spend my precious time? (Secret 10 again!)

When we lead in a purposeful way, taking time to determine how we will lead and what type of workplace we will create, we can make amazing things happen.

And just to be clear, even bad leaders manifest a design—but it's likely a bad design! Janice's leadership regimens almost guaranteed that she would struggle to get things done on time. Her workplace was designed to stress out her employees because they lacked a forum for effective planning, communication, and problem solving.

I bet you are wondering whether Janice improved. Unfortunately, Janice did not improve and was terminated. She was a sweet person and put in more hours than most, but she could not let go of her victim conversations long enough to take some coaching and redesign her leadership habits. Her manager gave her every opportunity to grow and change but she didn't. Incidentally, we worried a bit about how her team would react to her firing because she was well liked and she tried hard. I bet you can guess what happened. Janice's team was relieved and asked us what took us so long! They wished Janice well but knew she was in way over her head and was not coachable enough to change.

Our team members *want* effective leadership. They know you have a job to do, and they know that part of that job is to hold them accountable. They expect us to have grit when it comes to setting and reinforcing performance expectations. And they expect that we will have our acts together enough to make sure we can spend quality time with them. Our employees assume that we know how to design a workplace that works for all involved, and they are disappointed when we struggle to fit the important stuff into our busy day.

Secret 11: The secret to performance velocity is design. *Be intentional and create the world you seek.*

Our ability to cultivate highly accountable and engaged teams depends on what we do, how we do it, *and* how all the various parts fit together. If you want to see significant changes in accountability and engagement, you will be well served to look at the challenge from a designer's mindset. This may seem daunting, but it is not that tough as long as you bring together elements that are consistent with the 11 secrets and our model of accountability and engagement. Section II will help you do this.

CHAPTER TWELVE

The 11 Secrets for Cultivating Highly Accountable and Engaged Teams

Some of the secrets I've been sharing must seem like common sense and describe leadership practices you already use with your teams. I hope that a couple of these secrets helped you think a bit differently and that you are interested in learning how you can hone your approaches accordingly. Section II offers specific ideas and examples to do just that, so feel free to skip right to the parts that you think will benefit you most.

Here are the 11 secrets one more time, all together:

1. Using accountability systems to produce excellence is like taking a pocket knife to a gun fight. *Choose the right tools.*

2. To make accountability systems work, you may need to double the love. *Counterbalance the crud of change.*

3. Droning accountability measures and goals into people's heads puts them to sleep. *Don't repeat; resonate.*

4. The secret to accountability is grit. *Persevere.*

5. The secret to engagement is managerial love. *Take the initiative on behalf of someone else.*

6. Engagement is a gift you might not have earned. *Request humbly.*

7. Your most talented, highest performing employees might also be your least engaged. *Challenge even your best.*

8. You have a secret weapon you can use to engage others. *Be your brand of amazing.*

9. Surveys matter when you love lower scores more than higher ones. *Ask for the real stuff and let it affect how you lead.*

10. Most managers think time is precious but behave like it is worthless. *Do what matters.*

11. The secret to performance velocity is design. *Be intentional and create the world you seek.*

I like reviewing the whole list like this because it tells a story that holds together. In describing this overall leadership philosophy to someone the other day, I drew a diagram that you might find useful. Imagine a flip chart, with the following diagram (as an OD person, flip chart is my middle name):

Figure 12.1. Accountability/Engagement and Our Leadership Approach

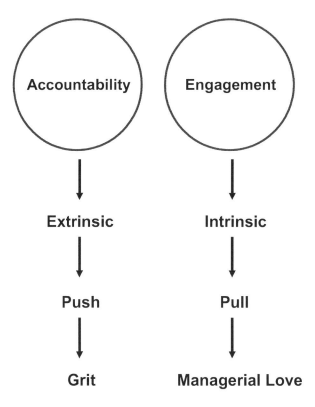

Here's the elevator speech that goes with the figure. Accountability is a managerial system based on extrinsic motivation—we hold people accountable. Because it is based on extrinsics, it is a push system, and therefore the secret to success is perseverance or grit. We must be consistent or the system will not work. Engagement, however, is a managerial system driven by performers and produced through intrinsic motivation. Because it is intrinsically based, it is a pull system, and therefore love is the secret to its success.

That's how I would sum up what we have explored so far. Are you ready to design a leadership regimen that will maximize accountability and engagement? Excellent. Let's head into Section II.

The Workshop

The Workshop

In Section I, I shared the 11 secrets you need to know to cultivate highly accountable and engaged teams, and I teased that more details would be revealed in Section II. Now it's time for me to deliver on those promises! I call this section "The Workshop" because it is structured to simulate the types of self-assessments, application discussions, and activities you might experience during a training workshop.

This section has two distinct parts: (1) self-assessments, and (2) tools and techniques that help address leadership capability that aligns with the secrets. In Chapter 13 on assessments, I offer several short exercises you can use to determine where you want to focus your developmental energies. I urge you to take a few moments to do the assessments; they will make clear the changes that will offer you the greatest benefit. And if you really want to dial in your diagnostic powers, ask your peers and team members to complete them as well. I have included some tips about how to do this.

The tools and techniques of Section II are dedicated to sharing specific, actionable ways you can put the secrets to work for you. Recommendations are organized into three major buckets—conversations, love, and design. Chapter 14 describes seven types of performance conversations that support accountability and engagement. Chapter 15 shares ten ways to show more managerial love. And Chapter 16 explores how leaders can use design principles to ensure they spend their time in ways that make the greatest impact.

Each chapter in Section II will share dozens of ways you can hone your daily and weekly regimens to increase performance velocity.

CHAPTER THIRTEEN

Self-Assessments

By this point in the book, you have a good understanding of accountability and engagement and the differences between these managerial systems. The following self-assessments will help you reflect on how you are currently leading and identify the changes you may want to make to your daily regimen. The four assessments cover

- Accountability

- Engagement

- Interplay between accountability and engagement

- Time

The assessments aren't rocket science, but they are very good for distinguishing what effective practices might look like on any given Tuesday at two o'clock. You will find them easy to complete but also very interesting. I encourage you to share them with your team members and peers to get their input as well. Their perspectives on how things are going may surprise you!

I once worked with a division chief executive officer (CEO) who I will call Jill. She was a brilliant professional but a little clueless when it came to the people stuff. Her leaders had a real conundrum on their hands. Jill had turned around the previously failing business unit to the point where it was now producing impressive numbers. This success was good for the employees in her unit because they did not have to worry about being shut down or downsized. At the same time, however, Jill's bosses were very concerned about the number of complaints they received from her managers who acknowledged that although she had saved the business, they hated working for her.

Jill's VP called me in to coach Jill. Let me just say that these types of coaching assignments are almost always doomed. You have to be a very strong person (in terms of emotional intelligence) to recover from and deal productively with having your boss force you to get coaching "or else." And, frankly, the types of leaders who get these ultimatums already tend to be low in emotional intelligence and self-awareness— that's why they need the coaching in the first place! I often have to spend the first month or so helping them get over the fact that they have been sent to coaching to be fixed.

But I digress, this is about Jill and the assessments. Jill had an ego the size of Texas, and she liked to think she was open, coachable, and eager to hear any feedback. I tested that by asking her if I could facilitate a session with her management team where they completed the accountability and engagement assessments (nearly identical to what's listed below). She eagerly said yes (but I could tell she was churning on the inside).

Given what I had been told by Jill's VP and my intuition from our first few coaching sessions, I predicted that Jill would score higher on accountability than engagement. She had turned the business around, after all, so there must be accountability measures in place.

I was wrong! She scored equally low on both assessments! I can still remember the shade of red she turned when I told her that her managers were not clear about their goals and priorities. "How dare they say this," she said, "we talk about these all the time."

My point in telling Jill's story here is that you never know what's clear and known until you ask. So, make sure you ask!

I know people love to hear the endings of stories, so I will tell you how things went with Jill. She was able to experience a few important epiphanies and improved enough to keep her job and build better relationships with the managers who reported to her. We also worked on making her management team stronger so they could stand up to her and help hold her more accountable. Was she ever a joy with which to work? No, the poor woman was entirely too serious. She retired three years later, and I am sure she is bossing around her shuffleboard partners right now.

Accountability Assessment

The first assessment focuses on the most important elements of an effective accountability system. That said, you may find that not every item is appropriate for your situation. Use this in the spirit it is offered—as a starting point for understanding how your managerial habits line up to produce highly accountable teams. Start by using the instrument as a *self*-assessment, reflecting on your own leadership capabilities. Using the same assessment, you can then take it a step further and ask individual team members or a small group of 4 or 5 members to reflect on your leadership.

To ensure that your team members feel comfortable sharing their feedback with you, set up the activity by saying something like this:

> I would like to continually improve our workplace and need your feedback to determine the best possible use of my time. Please work together (or in several small groups of 4-5) to complete these assessments. I will step out of the room so that you can talk freely!

Accountability Assessment

Directions: *Take five minutes to complete the quick assessment below. Indicate the best rating from columns A or B. Then, select one or two areas that you think need the most improvement (where attention would make the greatest difference) and indicate your choices in column C.*

Accountability Factors	A This is an area of STRENGTH	B This is an area of WEAKNESS	C This area should be a TOP PRIORITY
Team members know what the goals and priorities of the department/unit are (including behaviors and culture required).			
Team members understand their goals and performance expectations and know how you (the manager) define excellence for their roles.			
Goals for individuals and teams are routinely discussed and updated so that employees are clear about the work to focus on.			
Internal and external customer service standards are clear.			
Your (the manager's) actions match what you say is important.			
You (the manager) define excellence and communicate why it is so critical to the team's success.			
You (the manager) define and communicate what excellence looks like *in practice*.			
The team's performance in relation to its goals is understood and communicated.			
Each employee understands how he/she is doing in terms of performance to expectations.			
You (the manager) explain how performance will be measured and measure and manage performance based on this.			

You (the manager) handle performance issues without delay and ensure that struggling employees either improve or are removed from the team (or their role, if the issue is fit).			
Each employee meets with you (the manager) one-on-one at least quarterly to discuss performance, goals, and development.			
Performance evaluation discussions are thorough, participative, direct, and honest (ratings are real and accurate).			
New hire and promotion decisions reinforce the desired standards for excellence (for example, only team members who model the desired behaviors are promoted).			
This team is known for its ability to deliver results.			
Employees know how their roles support broader organizational goals and priorities.			
Accountability practices are administered consistently throughout the year, year after year (not flavor of the month).			

Engagement Assessment

The second assessment addresses engagement practices. As with the accountability assessment, start by taking the assessment yourself and then delve deeper by asking team members or peers to reflect on your engagement capabilities. The engagement assessment might be a bit tougher for you to share with your team members because it may feel more personal. But by definition, engagement is more personal. So feel free to change the wording on some of these assessment items if that helps, but please share it with your team. Doing so is an act of managerial love!

Engagement Assessment

Directions: *Take five minutes to complete the quick assessment below. Indicate the best rating from columns A or B. Then, select one or two areas that you think need the most improvement (where attention would make the greatest difference) and indicate your choices in column C.*

Engagement Factors	A This is an area of STRENGTH	B This is an area of WEAKNESS	C This should be a TOP PRIORITY
Team members feel cared for.			
Team members have strong and connecting relationships with one another.			
The relationships between the management team and employees are strong and connecting.			
Employees have the opportunity to make the unit better every day. You (the manager) encourage alternative ideas and reward proactive thinking.			
Although the team deals with some difficult situations, the workplace is fun.			
Employees believe that their work matters.			
You (the manager) are (the workplace is) as flexible as possible whenever possible.			
Partnerships between teams and other departments are productive and positive.			
It is common for employees to challenge ideas and initiate new solutions and suggestions for improvement.			
Most employees would report that their work requires them to learn new skills and approaches.			
Employees feel challenged (on the whole) and have at least one project/task that they feel intrinsically motivated to work on.			

Team members feel able to use their strengths at work.			
Team members feel that you (the manager) have their back and will do anything to help them do their best work.			
You (the manager) have discussed career and development goals with team members and have helped them plan for ways to work on things that most interest them.			
You (the manager) routinely change employees' roles to ensure their work will produce results.			
Assignments for high potential employees are made and changed to maximize their learning and impact to the organization. High performers and potentials are creatively used to fill emerging organizational needs.			
Employees seek out learning and knowledge wherever they can find it.			

Accountability and Engagement Assessment

This combined assessment includes just a few questions and is designed to help trigger your thoughts about how change is impacting your team. The responses elicited from this assessment will help you identify if there are external circumstances or changes that you need to consider and, perhaps, counterbalance. There are also items regarding being a lopsided manager to keep you thinking about balance. Most of us, by the way, are lopsided—stronger in accountability or in engagement. For example, I tend to skew toward engagement because I believe so strongly in the power of intrinsic motivation and have less faith in extrinsic rewards. So, when I take this assessment, it points to the need to kick up my resolve around providing regular performance conversations. As with the other assessments, take the assessment yourself first, and then ask your team members or peers to add their input through the instrument.

Accountability and Engagement Assessment

Directions: *Take five minutes to complete the quick assessment below. Indicate the best rating from columns A or B. Then, select one or two areas that you think need the most improvement (where attention would make the greatest difference) and indicate your choices in column C.*

	A	B	C
	Yes	No	This should be a TOP PRIORITY
We have had a lot of changes that are affecting how people feel about work.			
You (the manager) are concerned that new accountability systems are reducing team morale and/or engagement.			
The level of hassle in the workplace has gone up and is a concern.			
There is a lot of drama in the workplace (stress, team angst, burnout, etc.).			
Like many, you (the manager) are a lopsided leader: you likely emphasize accountability more than engagement.			
Like many, you (the manager) are a lopsided leader: you likely emphasize engagement more than accountability.			

The Time Audit

This basic time audit can be a powerful tool. I include it here because if you are the type of leader who is time challenged, you will find it difficult to do what it takes to cultivate highly accountable and engaged teams. In other words, time tends to be a barrier for many managers. I think you will find this self-assessment very helpful. This is a good one to share, too, especially with your manager.

Time Audit

Directions: *Take 10 minutes to complete Parts 1 and 2 below. Based on your answers, complete Part 3 and then experiment with making a few changes that might help you better use time.*

Part 1	Response
My broad goals, based on my manager's expectations, are…	
My most important priorities are…	
Am I spending enough time building accountability?	
Am I spending enough time cultivating engagement?	
The barriers getting in the way of my team's productivity are	
Planning and analysis that I need to complete in the next month includes	
I want to support/coach the following people this month	

Part 2	Response
Am I dissatisfied with the percentage of time I am dedicating to items covered in Part 1?	
The average number of hours a week I spend in meetings is	
Are these meetings a good use of my time? Why/why not?	
How successful are my employees? What have I done to optimize their performance?	
How clear is my team about which tasks are of highest priority?	

If I shared how I spend my time with my manager, peers, and employees, what would they likely say?	
How much time over the last week did I spend "doing" versus "managing"?	
How many hours do I work on average?	
Part 3	**Response**
Based on this audit, what goals should I set to improve how I spend time?	
What beliefs should I take on to help support these goals?	
What immediate actions can I take to begin using my time more wisely?	

Have you learned something about yourself? Perhaps these self-assessments have just confirmed what you already know about your leadership regimens, or perhaps they have pointed you in the direction of the changes that might help you most. Either way, it's important and beneficial information to use.

Now that you know what you need to change, you are ready for some ideas! The rest of the book is loaded with them, and I am sure you will find something that works for you.

CHAPTER FOURTEEN

Seven Performance Conversations

Dialogue is at the heart of performance velocity! As we explored in Section I, creating highly accountable and engaged teams is dependent upon your consistent use of sound practices. Leadership is a social act, and conversations are your currency for getting things done. So in this chapter, we will explore seven performance conversations you can use to strengthen accountability and support engagement. You will learn

- When to use expansion, inquiry, feedback, advocacy, evaluation, expectations, and intervention conversations and the key differences between each

- Fundamental steps to take when using each type of conversation

- Exercises and questions you can use to practice each type of conversation

As leaders, you have many opportunities to help team members improve their progress and performance. Each situation, however, is different in terms of what the performer most needs from you. Ask yourself these key questions: What does my employee most need from me to do his or her best work? Does she need guidance, or is the simple act of listening going to be most helpful? Does he need to hear candid feedback about what's not working, or will a catalytic question be the most effective source of help? Let's explore these and other questions.

The Seven Conversations—In Brief

Are there just seven types of conversations? No, there are hundreds, or more, I am sure. I have selected these specific examples because they represent a broad set of circumstances that will help you address both accountability and engagement and amp up performance velocity. These conversation types also maximize the benefit of both systems where applicable. Remember in Section I when I suggested that each leadership practice tends to support either accountability or engagement but not both? This is true for most of the things we do, but a few conversations have elements of both, and I want to make sure you are aware of them.

Please note that in exploring these seven performance conversations we will not be covering any specific formal disciplinary or documentation process (such as progressive discipline or corrective action policies). Your organization has a set practice it uses (if you don't know what your organization's practice is, have a chat with your HR folks). You will find, however, that the more you use the seven performance conversations listed below, the less you will need to use the formal disciplinary process. Why? Because the key reason that performance goes off the rails and needs to be dealt with harshly is that the manager has not been consistent and clear enough with regards to expectations, paths forward, and consequences.

> *The more you use the seven performance conversations, the less you will need to use the formal disciplinary process.*

Figure 14.1 lists the seven conversation types and how well they tend to serve accountability and engagement systems (caveat: when done properly). A "low" indication is not necessarily a bad thing, however, because some conversations are not designed to address both systems.

Figure 14.1

The Seven Performance Conversations and How They Impact Accountability and Engagement		
Conversation Type	**Reinforces Accountability**	**Supports Engagement**
Expansion: Purely developmental discussions that are designed to enliven the mind and increase curiosity, interest, and new learning.	Low	High
Inquiry: Catalytic conversations that help performers explore their goals and identify potential paths forward.	Medium	High
Feedback: Developmental coaching that affirms and/or shifts behaviors, builds self-awareness, and is not punitive. Managers offer open and helpful feedback as related to the performer's goals and intentions.	High	Low
Advocacy: Collaborative conversations that proactively make connections, solve problems, or remove barriers in a performer's way.	Medium	Medium
Evaluation: Summary discussions about performance in the past, coupled with future-oriented discussions about how to ensure an excellent future performance period.	High	Low
Expectations: Clarifying conversations about the reasons this performer/job/team/department exists and the contributions that the leader and organization expects from the performer both in terms of outcomes and approach.	High	Low
Intervention: Corrective conversations used to help a performer (who is not meeting an expectation) clearly understand the performance problem and what needs to change; most reactive, serious, and difficult of all the performance conversations.	High	Low

Do you begin to see how using this collection of performance conversations will help you cover a lot of leadership ground? Each has a place and proper use, and each can be wasted and misused. Each also differs in terms of how it makes the performer feel—an important consideration. As leaders, we need to be concerned about how our help is received—how our conversations impact others and how our messages "land." When you say something, what does it say about you?

Some of these conversations will come more naturally to you based on your behavioral tendencies (style) and your previous management experiences. To effectively use the seven conversations, therefore, you might need to move outside of your comfort zone in some circumstances.

Let's explore each conversation in more detail. We will examine their purpose, strengths/weaknesses, whether they serve to aid accountability or engagement, the leader's role and posture in conducting them (who should show up), when to use them, how to start them, and the pitfalls to avoid.

Expansion Conversations

WHAT: Expansion conversations are purely developmental discussions designed to enliven the mind and increase curiosity, interest, and new learning. They increase challenge and personal growth but are often put off or not conducted due to time constraints because they seem a luxury or optional. For your team members, however, these conversations are very important and may be a significant contributing factor as to whether and how fully they engage.

ACCOUNTABILITY OR ENGAGEMENT? This type of conversation serves the engagement environment. Don't even try to address the topic of accountability during an expansion discussion; doing so will likely ruin the intrinsically motivating aspects of this precious leadership tool. Trust me on this!

WHO SHOULD SHOW UP: For this conversation, the leader is playful, open, and fascinated. You will not be serving your agenda here, so you have no particular goal that you are advocating apart from igniting learning (pull, not push). The leader does not assert control over the conversation—the performer does.

WHEN TO USE: Expansion conversations should occur both regularly and as needed to ensure that your team members are actively and routinely thinking and exploring new concepts or approaches (even if for only a few moments each week). This conversation is appropriate to use with individuals or groups

- When performers seem stuck, bored, or burned out, but not overwhelmed

- When performers are doing extraordinary work and are ready for some mental stimulation

- When a team needs to work together to innovate

- When your industry/function/organization is experiencing a lot of change and you want to be proactive in ensuring your team members stay current (or even on the edge)

HOW TO APPROACH THE CONVERSATION: Use these opening lines to help you start the conversation:

- Javier, I know you admire the work of Lucy Ming, and I noticed she is speaking in town. Why don't we get a group of folks to attend the talk and then have a reflections discussion afterward? Would you be interested in leading this?

- I sent a link to the white paper on the quality award winners and asked you to underline ideas that you thought we might be able to learn from. Let's explore those....

- What's a crazy idea that just might work? The crazier the better....

- Who would you most like to work with or learn from?

PITFALLS TO AVOID: Because this conversation is the most creative and should be driven by performers, the most common pitfall for managers is getting in the way of the performer's learning and interest. If done well, this type of conversation is not predictable because pull learning is nonlinear and chaotic. Behaviors that might reduce discovery include the following:

- Pushing the idea because you think the employee "ought" to be interested in this. He or she might be interested but might not be interested right now.

- Trying to tie everything to a specific job task, goal, or expected outcome. Let the learning happen, and the team member(s) will make the connection to their work on their own.

- Failing to think beyond your department. Expansive conversations, by definition, expand our thinking and influences. Go broad. I once took a team to a Cirque du Soleil show for the jolt to our inventiveness. It was great.

Expansion Exercise—Try Something New

Instructions: Small group exercise—30 minutes every two weeks (or during your team staff meetings, whenever they occur).

One of the easiest ways to ignite others and ensure you don't inadvertently muck up this expansion exercise by over-controlling it (if you are a recovering control freak like me, you might need extra help) is to design it so that others must lead. It's a simple and amazingly effective practice that always works.

Tell your team that you want to dedicate 30 minutes of every team meeting to learning something new. At each meeting, a different team member will select something to share that he or she thinks is interesting and then the group will discuss it. It might be a blog post, a video, a model, a science experiment, a song, or whatever! It could even be a guest speaker. Offer to go first so that everyone will have time to plan, and then suggest that the order of who goes next be alphabetical (people can switch with each other if they need to).

Since you are going first, do something "out there" that will show the team that anything goes. Share a poem and why it inspires you. Talk about the person you admire most. Have them construct atoms made of cheese. In other words, do something that will serve to broaden the possibilities for what your team does. Trust me on this—it will set a great tone.

To ensure that you show that the expansion exercise is important, put it first on the agenda. There are two reasons to do this. First, placed at the top of the agenda it won't get bumped. Schedule it last and you will end up cutting into your team member's time and that will dampen their enthusiasm. Second, this exercise will prime their brains and put them in a great mood, making the rest of your meeting more productive.

Brainstorm five potential ideas for your starter expansion discussion below:

1. _____

2. _____

3. _____

4. _____

5. _____

Inquiry Conversations

WHAT: Catalytic conversations allow performers to explore their goals, intentions, plans, barriers, or options. (Note that a catalyst makes things easier.) The leader asks great questions and listens—more listening than talking! The light bulb of inspiration goes on as a result of the inquiry, not because the leader has given the performer an answer. This conversation type shares some qualities with the expansion conversation but is more goal oriented.

ACCOUNTABILITY OR ENGAGEMENT? This type of conversation offers you the chance to heighten both accountability and engagement, but more so engagement because the primary motivational force you will tap into is intrinsic. This is not a rigorous discussion where you provide feedback or render a judgment about performance.

WHO SHOULD SHOW UP: The leader is caring, interested, and driven to help. The leader does not assert control over the conversation—the performer is in control.

WHEN TO USE: Inquiry conversations are highly engaging and useful, so use them often. This conversation is appropriate when performers have a goal or interest and express some commitment and ownership:

- When performers are stuck and are not sure how to move forward

- When performers are learning new tasks or skills

- When a performer is enthusiastic about a new idea, or when you are working with him or her on creating a plan for how to approach his or her work

- Day-to-day conversations with team members

HOW TO APPROACH THE CONVERSATION: Use these opening lines as examples to help you start the conversation:

- What are your burning questions about this idea?

- Would it be helpful if we talked through your ideas and questions about this?

- I don't want to get in the way of your creativity or inadvertently squash new ideas, so why don't you start by telling me where things stand and where you want to head with the plan/idea/goal?

- I can see that you have a lot of interest in and ownership for this project. Is there anything getting in your way?

- You have amazing talents. If I asked you for the top three ways you think you could contribute to the organization—and time and resources were not a barrier—what would you list?

PITFALLS TO AVOID: Because this conversation should be catalytic, the most common pitfall for managers is getting in the way of the performer's progress and discovery. Behaviors that might reduce progress and discovery include the following:

- *Over-sharing your story:* Think: "This is not about me." You might have a great story to share, but please keep it brief. There is a difference between sharing and making a contribution (contributions add something), and remember that not all stories are as helpful as we might believe. Even if the performer asks you to share an example, be brief and focus on the most salient points. If he or she wants to hear more, he or she will ask follow-up questions.

- *Assigning value and judgment:* Inquiry conversations are open explorations, and you will erode the performer's energy and interest in the conversation if you come across in a way that makes him or her feel like you are judging the person or the idea.

- *Allowing your personal history to influence the conversation:* Our experience is invaluable, but it can also become a barrier to good inquiry. Statements like "We tried that and it did not work" deflate the conversation. Also, our history serves to filter our perceptions and we might not see or consider new ideas that lie outside our frame of reference or comfort zone.

Inquiry Exercise—What Does Great Inquiry Look Like?

Instructions: Small group exercise—20 minutes total.

Part 1. Examples of questions you might use during an inquiry conversation are listed below. Take 5 minutes to identify four characteristics that these questions share:

- Question: If time and resources were not an issue, what would you do?

- Question: Who would be the best person with whom you could partner on this?

- Question: There are obviously lots of barriers you are dealing with, but what is the key constraint slowing things down?
- Question: How would you define a grand-slam home run for this project over the next six months?
- Question: What's the wildest idea that just might work?

Characteristics of the above questions:

1. _____

2. _____

3. _____

4. _____

Part 2. Use these questions as idea starters and create TWO NEW questions for EACH of three situations listed below. Your questions should be catalytic and have the potential to open up dialogue. Take 10 minutes to do this.

A. Performer who is struggling with a problem that involves gaining support from others:

Question 1: _____

Question 2: _____

B. Performer who is struggling to determine how to improve a regular work process:

Question 1: _____

Question 2: _____

C. Performer who is creating a work plan for an important departmental goal or initiative:

Question 1: _____

Question 2: _____

Feedback Conversations

WHAT: Feedback conversations are developmental and improve the performer's self-awareness. The performer should drive this conversation and ask for the feedback. The feedback is based on your observations and should be delivered in a way that reduces resistance and defensiveness as well as improves coachability. This feedback should be sought by the performer—they should want to hear it (or they won't really hear it). As a leader, you might not think that performers "ask" for feedback very often, but they will if you create an environment where seeking it is encouraged and where being open is safe and constructive.

ACCOUNTABILITY OR ENGAGEMENT? This type of conversation primarily serves building accountability because it is specifically focused on sharing the outcome of some performance and is extrinsically motivating. Even when the feedback is requested, you are the one rendering an evaluative opinion about something. It is possible that the performers might experience an epiphany that affects their engagement, but this is not often the case. If anything, feedback tends to temporarily reduce engagement (because most of us feel uncomfortable receiving feedback).

WHO SHOULD SHOW UP: The leader is open, nonjudgmental, and positive and has no particular goal other than to help through sharing an observation. Feedback is best when the leader does not assert control over the conversation, but it is common that the performer will feel like you are driving it. Be flexible and don't push the conversation if the performer is not coachable at the time you approach him or her (we are all coachable at times and uncoachable at others).

WHEN TO USE: The feedback conversation should be used when the performer is interested in learning and growing and when overall performance is not a concern (use intervention conversations to address performance problems). We all need feedback to do our best work and to address minor issues. This everyday coaching should not feel like punishment or failure.

HOW TO APPROACH THE CONVERSATION: To begin a feedback conversation, start with a genuine offer (not a set up for an intervention—it is fine if they don't take you up on the feedback). These openers should help you get started:

- I know you are working on your development plan and you mentioned that you would like to learn more about how better to sell your ideas. I would be happy to share any observations I have about your current approach and what I have seen others do that did and didn't work well.

- (Performer expresses frustration about how meetings turn out.) As you know, I think you are doing a great job. I am not concerned at all. If you would like some specific feedback about your presentation style, I would be happy to share my observations anytime.

PITFALLS TO AVOID: Many managers struggle with the difference between feedback conversations and interventions. Feedback conversations are developmental and deal with performance that might not be perfect but is not a problem. Be sure your offer of feedback does not come across as

- *Threats:* Avoid thinly veiled threats that sound like "fix this or else ____."

- *Advice:* Most people are not interested in advice. Never ask: "Can I give you some advice?"

- *Overly General:* Feedback should be specific. Avoid generalizations like: "You seem to be overwhelmed all the time," "You're not a people person," or "You are a negative person."

- *Intervention:* If it is not a problem but just fine-tuning, say so. Put the performer at ease. Never say "You need to do better," during a feedback conversation. Also avoid saying "I know you have some personal challenges, but you are letting your team member's down." (This approach would be devastating and would diminish the performer's ownership of the opportunity for improvement.)

- *Insensitive:* Adjust your feedback so that the performer can hear it (be cognizant of his or her communication preferences). Just because feedback is factual does not make it effective.

Feedback Exercise—Performer-Driven Feedback

Feedback conversations are most successful when the performer seeks the feedback. You do not want to come across as pushy or in a way that sounds like you are trying to give him or her advice. So how does a manager create the environment where feedback will be sought by the performer?

Your challenge: Imagine that you are having a conversation with one of your team members, Sally. You think some feedback might help her with a goal she seems very interested in accomplishing. How do you start the conversation without taking over too much control? Create ten potential conversation lead-in statements that follow these four rules:

- Avoid the appearance of offering advice. Don't ask: "Can I give you some advice?"—even in disguise.

- Strive to come across as service oriented rather than "managing."

- Focus on being developmental, not judgmental.

- Initiate the conversation, but let the performer drive it (resist the temptation to control).

1. _____

2. _____

3. _____

4. _____

5. _____

6. _____

7. _____

8. _____

9. _____

10. _____

Advocacy Conversations

WHAT: Advocacy conversations seek to help performers get unstuck or improve progress. The leader asks what he or she can do to be of most help to the performer and acts as an enabler. Share ideas and options, but ultimately agree to assist in the way that the performer thinks will make the greatest difference. This conversation, when done well, increases energy and motivation because it feels great to be moving forward again.

ACCOUNTABILITY OR ENGAGEMENT? This type of conversation offers a medium level of impact on both accountability and engagement. Accountability goals are served because the focus is on a current task or goal. Engagement is supported because progress is one of the most powerful motivators and makes us feel more successful. Done well, these conversations are quick, easy, and fabulous.

Consider this excerpt from a *Harvard Business Review* article titled "What Really Motivates Workers," by Teresa M. Amabile and Steven J. Kramer:

> In a recent survey we invited more than 600 managers from dozens of companies to rank the impact on employee motivation and emotions of five workplace factors commonly considered significant: recognition, incentives, interpersonal support, support for making progress, and clear goals. "Recognition for good work (either public or private)" came out number one. Unfortunately, those managers are wrong.

Amabile and Kramer completed a multiyear study in which participants kept daily journals (over 12,000 journal entries). The authors found that the top motivator for employees was progress. Employees felt more motivated and positive on days when they were able to get something done, move past barriers, or make meaningful headway. As Amabile and Kramer discovered, "Making progress in one's work—even incremental progress—is more frequently associated with positive emotions and high motivation than any other workday event."

Advocacy conversations are powerful and important. Use them often!

WHO SHOULD SHOW UP: The leader is open, ready to offer ideas, and able to help. You come with ideas for solutions but do not take over the conversation—let the performer decide how he or she would most like you to help. It is important to be service minded for this conversation because you might need to do something on the performer's behalf (make a call, talk to someone, bring people together, facilitate a decision, and so on).

WHEN TO USE: Advocacy conversations are useful anytime you think you might be able to help remove a barrier for a performer or facilitate a connection that will help the performer move forward.

HOW TO APPROACH THE CONVERSATION: The advocacy conversation starts with an offer and is service oriented. For example, you might say the following:

- You mentioned that you were having a hard time finding good data. Would you like me to set up a meeting so that you can talk with an analyst to see if he or she can help?

- I know you are waiting on a decision from the marketing department. Let me know if you would like me to talk with Javiar to see what's holding things up.

- I know you are interested in using social media to improve project communication, and I got this flier for a local workshop that looks good and might help you decide if that's a good avenue. Would you like to attend?

PITFALLS TO AVOID: The most common pitfall for advocacy conversations occurs when the leader combines help with too much control. You do not want to take over the problem or opportunity; your involvement should not diminish the ownership the performer feels for the work. In addition, be careful not to

- *Help too much.* Offer assistance that is helpful and requested, but then let the performer handle things.

- *Take credit.* Advocacy is help, but the performer is still doing (or leading) the work.

- *Help when it's not wanted.* Don't step in too early or before the performer has asked for help.

Double The Love 95

Advocacy Exercise—20 Ways to Be an Advocate

Instructions: Below is a list of 20 ways leaders can be advocates. Take a look at the list and then identify two **real** and **specific** ways you could offer help to an employee, peer, or manager **this week**.

1. Make a call on Sally's behalf.
2. Make an introduction.
3. Meet with someone to request a decision.
4. Offer a book or other resource.
5. Do one of Sally's tasks so that she can focus.
6. Offer to pick up lunch for Sally.
7. Submit Sally's name for a promotion/project/training.
8. Show active support during a team meeting.
9. Make a decision that removes a barrier.
10. Eliminate pesky steps or tasks.
11. Tutor Sally during lunch.
12. Suggest Sally work from home or in a quiet meeting room.
13. Offer to proof or review an initial draft.
14. Offer to speak to Sally's team.
15. Temporarily change Sally's role or goals.
16. Offer to help Sally.
17. Make a reverse request (a request on behalf of Sally).
18. Offer to "loan" another team member to Sally's project.
19. Give Sally permission to skip one or more meetings.
20. Ask each member to share requests for help at each staff meeting to create a departmental culture of community.

Two ways I can be an advocate this week:

1. _____

2. _____

Evaluation Conversations

WHAT: Evaluation conversations are summary discussions about performance in the past, coupled with future-oriented discussions about how to ensure an excellent future performance period. Most organizations use annual performance evaluation processes, and some also have leaders conduct mini-evaluations every six months. I will not address specific design features of evaluation processes here but rather the characteristics of the evaluation discussion that will make these conversations more successful. The key characteristic that distinguishes effective from ineffective evaluations is meaning. Don't waste your time and your performer's time detailing a laundry list of the activities and tasks he or she completed. This is not a time to focus on activity. Instead, summarize the contributions of the performer. In what ways did he or she make an impact? This focus will best prepare you for the coming year (which is the purpose of the evaluation). The evaluation should feel like a report about contribution, not an inventory of actions.

ACCOUNTABILITY OR ENGAGEMENT? This type of conversation is a core part of the accountability system and that's the performance it impacts most. Because the manager is rendering a judgment (even when the employee is asked to do a self-review, the manager gets to make the final assessment), it is an extrinsic motivator and therefore a push activity. The future-oriented part has some qualities that might stir engagement a bit but not very much. One caveat is that the more that you focus on summarizing the performer's contribution, the more engaging the conversation will feel because we all want to believe we make a difference and knowing that we did makes us feel warm and fuzzy inside.

WHO SHOULD SHOW UP: The leader needs to be clear, efficient, and open. And the most important characteristic that improves this conversation is preparation and previous update discussions. In other words, it is important that you have done your homework and that there are no surprises because the performer has received lots of performance feedback throughout the year. The leader also needs to be brave enough to be honest. I am going to assume that you have been providing feedback on specific situations all year, but it is doubly hard for leaders to summarize performance in ways that will disappoint or anger the performer. Hopefully you won't need to do that very often, but please be honest when and if the time comes. (I have observed that many leaders are not truthful on performance evaluations, especially if merit raises are attached to the performance evaluation process. It is better to not do them at all than to low-ball the feedback.)

WHEN TO USE: Evaluation conversations are appropriate when you want to assess and communicate performance for a defined period of time. Use them

- When the performance period is over (usually a year)

- When performers have accomplished a project or major goal

- When a performer is transitioning from one role to another within the organization

HOW TO APPROACH THE CONVERSATION: Use these examples of opening lines to help you get the conversation started:

- I am glad we can take this time to discuss how things have been going. I would not expect there to be any surprises, since we have been talking all year long….

- The evaluation does not uncover new information, but it allows us to take some time to reflect on the previous year and plan for the coming year, and I think that's a valuable thing to do.

- Bill, I want to take a few moments to acknowledge all the things you have accomplished this year, and then I want to spend some time clarifying what the coming year will hold and get your thoughts on all that and areas where you might want to grow.

PITFALLS TO AVOID: Because this conversation is generally dreaded by all parties, you will need to work extra hard to make it worthwhile. Behaviors that reduce the value of this conversation type include the following

- *Blindsiding the performer.* I know I have stressed this many times already, but it is worth saying again: The evaluation should contain no surprises!

- *Spending too much time summarizing past performance and not enough looking forward.* If your goal is to improve accountability (and it is), you can only do this on future performance so spend at least 50 percent of the time looking forward.

- *Not getting to the right point.* It is important to share specifics, but only when those details are meaningful. In the evaluation conversation, you want to summarize the contributions of the performer, not just list what he or she did. This is not an inventory of activity; it is a report on impact.

- *Failing to get your employee's input.* Although this is a push system (extrinsically motivating), ask your employees to do a self-review to help calibrate your perceptions and make sure you have the correct information.

- *Using emotionally charged words.* Accountability practices, in general, and the evaluation discussion, in specific, are best served when you can reduce any mental garbage that will get in the way of good and clear communication. I'm not suggesting that you shouldn't high five your best performers, but I would urge you to refrain from telling an employee she has a "bad attitude." This kind of emotionally charged phrase can run the discussion off the tracks.

Evaluation Exercise—Getting to the Right Point

The challenge with the evaluation discussion is that you want to share specifics from the past year, and you also want to save at least half the time to discuss the coming year. I have seen many leaders struggle with this, spending most of their time summarizing the past year in ways that are not useful. Remember, the evaluation discussion should focus on contribution, not activity. To help you discern the difference, consider the two statements that follow (note: one defines what the performer did; the other describes her impact):

Statement 1: Shino, under the goal of leading the conversion project, you completed the project on time, the project implementation team met all its major milestones, and the conversion is running at acceptable efficiencies. Great work!

Statement 2: Shino, let's talk about the conversion project. You led the team so that all the key metrics were met, which is terrific. You made a positive impact with your resilience regarding how the team came together and dealt with several setbacks. And you helped the team stay positive and productive when many of the team members were getting discouraged. You helped them do better and feel better, which will benefit not just the conversion project but projects in the future. Great work!

Do you see the difference? Statement 1 defines only what the performer did (activity), whereas statement 2 describes her impact (contribution).

This is a positive example, and oddly enough I think leaders struggle more with very good performance. I have thought about why this is. When we are faced with a disappointing review, we tend to prepare more and get advice from our managers and HR. When we are evaluating great performance, however, we tend to think we can wing it and not prepare as much. We end up falling back on superlative generalizations like: "Shino, you are great, no issues here at all." Your best performers already know there are no issues, so don't waste their time meandering through the evaluation with generalized compliments. Take the time to articulate the unique and valuable contributions each performer made.

Let's practice! I have listed three writing prompts for you below. Write two sample descriptions for each, just like I did with the Shino example above. This will help you distinguish between meaningless dribble about checklist items and effective evaluation conversations that will help drive top performance in the coming year.

1. Feedback about a process improvement goal:

Activity: _____

Contribution: _____

2. Feedback about a customer service goal:

Activity: _____

Contribution: _____

3. Feedback about a quality improvement goal:

Activity: _____

Contribution: _____

Expectations Conversations

WHAT: Expectations conversations clarify the reasons this performer/job/team/department exists and the contributions that the leader and organization expect from the performer both in terms of outcomes and approach. Expectations exist in several layers or aspects of performance. For example, there's what the performer is being asked to accomplish, the culture and values that the performer is expected to represent, and the approaches or practices leaders expect the performer to use. It is common that leaders articulate surface-level goals but fail to clarify expectations regarding how the work ought to be done. Most performance issues are not problems of volume; they tend to be problems of approach and values. Improving expectations conversations is one of the best ways to prevent performance issues from occurring.

ACCOUNTABILITY OR ENGAGEMENT? This type of conversation is a core part of your accountability system. Done well, you might spark a bit of engagement, but this conversation is a push activity and extrinsically motivating, so it is primarily about accountability.

WHO SHOULD SHOW UP: The leader needs to be clear and thorough but not prescriptive. Does this sound like a contradiction? It is important to describe your expectations fully and on many layers but not tell performers exactly how they should get the job done. We want clarity—not micromanagement—and there is a big difference between the two.

WHEN TO USE: Expectations conversations are among the most important for building highly accountable teams. Specifically, use expectations conversations

- When performers are starting a new performance period or project

- Quarterly or monthly to update and reinforce expectations

- When a performer seems off track and you think he or she might not fully understand what you expect

- Regularly with your team to reinforce your most important expectations

HOW TO ARTICULATE EXPECTATIONS: Here are several sample expectations statements of varying effectiveness. Notice how the better examples are more specific without being prescriptive. For example, the last item sets the expectation that the performer will ensure that all key stakeholders are well informed of the project's progress. It does not stipulate when the communication will occur, by whom, or what information will be shared—that would be too prescriptive (that is, micromanaging).

- *Poor example:* Complete the ABC project on time and budget.

- *Slightly better example:* Lead the ABC project team to successful completion of all measures of success and in ways that build stronger partnerships and end-user adoption of the new system.

- *Poor example:* Reduce accounting errors.

- *Still poor example*: Reduce errors by 10 percent.

- *Better example:* Lead a cross-functional team that finds and implements ways to reduce accounting errors by 10 percent or more. Create an environment where errors will be discussed and addressed positively and proactively as a part of the culture through emphasizing mutual support, openness, a learning mindset, and broad participation. We want people to own improving their error rates and feel comfortable being open about errors and supporting each other to learn better practices.

- *Poor example:* Create and deliver the XYZ project by end of year, on budget.

- *Better example:* Manage the project so that the team completes it by _____ and within the agreed to budget of _____. Lead the project team so that members are always aware of their individual and collective progress toward the goals. Foster positive communication and collaboration on the project team and with internal customers. Keep senior management up-to-date on the project, including successes, obstacles, and challenges. Proactively enlist leadership support in removing barriers to the project's completion. When successfully implemented, this project will revolutionize the way we interact with community leaders and internal partners.

PITFALLS TO AVOID: Because expectations conversations are critical for setting your accountability system up for success, it is important to do them well. Behaviors that might reduce performer clarity include the following:

- *Using wimpy or general statements.* Share expectations in clear, specific, and resolute terms. Cover the what, the how, and the key contributions expected.

- *Using statements that are too emotionally charged.* To reduce the emotional content of the discussion, express expectations in a matter-of-fact manner. An expectations conversation should not become a sermon, a plea, or a sales pitch.

- *Being too prescriptive.* Focus on the essential outcome—but allow latitude on how to get there.

- *Failing to discuss all important expectations.* Never assume that expectations are clear.

Expectations Exercise—Including Enough Information

Instructions: Check out the two lists below and then sketch out an expectations conversation for one of your team members. It might seem like a lot to plan for, but I promise you that the time you spend up front clarifying expectations will be well worth it.

The usual expectations conversations often include expectations about

- Required tasks

- Project work

- Regular and ongoing work that the employee is responsible for

- Types of tasks this person should own

- How the employee will communicate questions and problems to the manager

More effective expectations conversations also include expectations about

- How the performer should contribute to identifying and solving problems.

- How the performer will represent their function and the company.

- Generating new ideas and improving results.

- How the performer should analyze and manage organizational resources (for example: staff, finances, and equipment).

- How the performer will manage employees.

- Business relationships the performer should maintain and develop.

- Deadlines, execution, and results.

- Judgment and decisions.

- Meeting preparedness and participation.

- Planning and communicating work.

- How the performer needs to improve his or her performance. For example, "Over the next year, I would like to see you more closely manage productivity in the A/P area and improve the speed and accuracy of the employees of that group. This is an area where you have not been as attentive or effective."

The second list of discussion topics may seem long, but it is necessary to ensure that each person fully understands what he or she is expected to accomplish. And think about it, where do the issues occur—with items on the first list or the second? More often, performance associated with the second list is the source of the struggle or conflict.

Now it is your turn to use these lists to sketch out an expectations conversation for one of your employees.

_____

_____

_____

_____

Intervention Conversations

WHAT: Intervention conversations are corrective, designed to stop an unproductive practice or result and change the performer's behaviors for the better. They are used when a leader needs to intervene because a performer is not meeting expectations in one or more ways. The intervention conversation is intended to get performers back on track.

ACCOUNTABILITY OR ENGAGEMENT? This type of conversation is an accountability conversation. It is a push discussion and extrinsically motivating. You are not addressing engagement with the intervention conversation.

WHO SHOULD SHOW UP: The leader is in control and needs to have the courage to be clear, candid, and specific. You will also show that you care by being brief, focused, and supportive.

WHEN TO USE: Intervention conversations are an important tool that leaders will need to use on occasion. While it is preferable to use the other performance conversations that prevent performance problems from occurring, they might not be adequate. An intervention conversation is serious, usually addressing certain types of performance:

- *Inappropriate:* violation of work rules, interpersonal interactions that adversely impact others and productivity, or poor customer service

- *Impermissible:* violation of the code of conduct or workplace expectations

- *Illegal:* violation of ethics, contributing to hostile workplace

HOW TO APPROACH THE CONVERSATION: Please note that you may need to discuss this issue with your HR partner to get his or her guidance before initiating an intervention conversation. Use these openers to help you start the conversation:

- I need to talk about your interactions with the team, specifically Sally, during your project presentation to the executive team.

- John, we have discussed your team communications in the past, and I want to spend some time on this again now. Here is what I have observed since we last spoke . . . .

- Layne, I could tell from the look on your face that you knew that what you did yesterday was not the right response to the problem. Am I correct? I want to discuss what happened and why . . . .

PITFALLS TO AVOID: Interventions are difficult conversations. As the leader, you need to maintain control while at the same time help the performer take ownership of his or her issue and its solution. Here are some common pitfalls to avoid:

- *Don't ease in or be indirect.* There are two reasons why this approach is a pitfall. First, you want to focus on the issue, not other topics. Second, performers sense that you are trying to get to a point and wish you would get there more quickly (it is not kind to drag it out). Don't say, "How did the meeting go"? "How was your vacation?"

- *Don't assume you know the performer's intention and don't give it too much weight.* Good intentions (most of us have good intentions) do not excuse a poor impact. This sentence is filled with emotive language and assumptions, "Your efforts to intimidate me and control others will not be tolerated."

- *Don't act like you are conducting an investigation, unless you are, and then that's a whole different conversation and should be led by your HR partner.* Avoid legal language such as "You could be in a lot trouble and I will be talking to other witnesses."

- *Don't present your conclusions as the truth.* Don't exaggerate by using words like "always" and "never," which are inflammatory and inaccurate. Avoid statements such as "You always leave the tools in the truck and not in the tool room" or "You never submit your timesheet on time."

- *Don't skip the follow-up step.* One conversation is unlikely to solve the problem. The performer's response is just the beginning. He or she will go back to his or her workplace and mull over the conversation. New, additional, or different emotions and opinions will likely surface.

In addition to these common pitfalls, there are three other pitfalls that are critically important to avoid:

- *Attributing*: "You are new to group, which explains your line of questioning."

- *Blaming*: "Your lack of experience has put a burden on a usually high-performing group."

- *Judging*: "It is obvious to everyone that you are hostile and uncooperative."

Intervention Exercise—Getting the Best Result from a Corrective Conversation

Instructions: To get the best result from an intervention conversation, you need to start strong and clear. Using the guidelines in this chapter, sketch out an opening line for the following situations.

A. George had a meltdown, screamed at you, and then stormed out of the meeting room:

_____

_____

B. Beverly has great technical skills but is uncooperative, negative, and short tempered with team members:

_____

_____

C. Sam did not get the report out on time; this is the third time he has missed an important deadline and impacted many others who relied on getting the information in time:

_____

_____

Conclusion

Now that we've explored the seven performance discussions, start using them more deliberately and noticing which you use often and which you should add to your leadership regimen. While it is not important that you label each discussion with the titles I have given them here, it is helpful to distinguish the characteristics of each and understand what each conversation is designed to produce in terms of accountability and engagement (and what it will NOT do). In my experience, leaders tend to favor a couple types of conversations and underutilize others.

If you want to increase accountability, use the performance conversations that promote accountability. Ditto if you want to improve the likelihood that your employees will engage more fully in their work.

In the next chapter , we will switch gears to focus on ways we can give more managerial LOVE.

CHAPTER FIFTEEN

Ten Ways to Show Managerial Love

Oh, how much fun we will have in this chapter! That's the way it's got to be because we are talking about managerial love—taking initiative on the behalf of someone else. There are trillions of ways to do this, but I am going to share ten of my favorites here. As we explored in Section I, managerial love is the key to engaging your employees and it can mean many things. We show love when we provide a challenge, when we reduce a burden, when we make someone smile, and when we build caring connections between people. So sit down, grab a cup of coffee, and let's talk love for a moment.

If you are a regular reader of my blog, *Management Craft*, you know that I have written a lot about great leaders and the things they do to make the workplace more wonderful. I have also used the blog to share my personal epiphanies and observations about what works and what doesn't. I am fascinated with the things we can do to jazz up our workplaces to help everyone feel more alive doing "work." It's the ultimate four-letter word.

When planning this chapter, I remembered something a very wise man once said: "Your context needs to match your intentions." The wise man is the brilliant leadership guru Peter Block, and he shared this idea at a conference I attended. He urged us to be deliberate about the way we communicate and the environment we establish to ensure that it all speaks the same message. What this means is that a chapter about love must be emotional and exciting. Cool. Yikes!

To that end (now there is a phrase that does not belong in an engaging chapter), I have scoured the archives of *Management Craft* and selected emotional and exciting posts that illustrate ten ways to show managerial love. After each post, I offer a few pointers you can use to put the tip into play (noticed I did not say, "implement the recommendation," as this would be far too stodgy and contextually out of alignment).

10 Ways to Show Managerial Love

1. Show you believe in them.
2. Learn from them.
3. Help them do what they love most.
4. Encourage new bravery.
5. Help them create an exciting new goal.
6. Listen deeply.
7. Be a "Yes" person.
8. Blast away hassles that distract them.
9. Put more BANG! and WOW! into meetings.
10. Be interested in them.

Looks like a fun list, doesn't it? I hope these ideas fill you with more ideas and that you give them a try. Going back to our secret about using your strengths (Secret 8), select the tips that seem most "like you." Or, stretch yourself and select the tips that are not at all like you! As long as you are honest in your effort, you will make a positive impression on employee engagement. I know it!

1. Show You Believe in Them

I wrote the first blog post for this way to show managerial love back in 2009 and then reflected on it again in 2012; I have included both posts here. Although these posts are written from the mindset of our own mojo (or lack of mojo), imagine how you might help your team members feel concurrently flawed and fabulous and use this energy to get on track with the work that is most important to them.

You Are Amazing Even If Today You Are Off Course, December 30, 2009

I thought I would end the year's blog postings on a high note and with a call for self-forgiveness (continuing the theme of best mind forward) as a vehicle for refocusing on generating the life and work you desire.

You are amazing. I know this! If you and I enjoyed a chat over foaming lattes, I am sure that your greatness would shine brightly and I would find your hopes and dreams inspiring. Everyone I meet possesses clear and special talents. I love to discover the source of a person's passions and am fascinated by our diverse natures.

Every night on the TV, we see people at their best and more often at their worst (crime shows, reality TV, Jerry Springer). If everyone is amazing, what's going on? I think that stress and the dizzying circumstances of our lives can push us off course. We know this is not how things ought to be. We know that we have something greater and more compelling to offer the world. Even so, we get farther off course with each mismatched turn.

You are amazing even if today you are off course. You have the potential to contribute to society and live a wonderful and fulfilling life. You can get back on track. I work with many people who choose to stop moving in the wrong direction and see a new set of possibilities. They flap their butterfly wings fast and furious, manifesting joy and wonder along the way. They ooze exuberance and become flexibly strong, like a tall Sequoia tree swaying in the wind. An awesome force of nature. What's your goal? Do you need an adjustment?

You can start right now:

- What can I do in the next 12 hours to get unstuck? (Do one big or five tiny things then rejoice.)

- Which is more powerful—physical or mental barriers? (Hint: it's likely mental—obliterate the barriers by taking on a new perspective.)

- What two things can I do for the next five days to get back on track?

Isn't it more complex than this? Yes, of course it is, but if you act like it isn't—guess what? It will become simpler. And yes, this is familiar. To generate breakthroughs, Define–Ask–Act–Create:

- *Define:* Define goals that inspire you and share them broadly.

- *Ask:* Make requests that move things forward.

- *Act:* Take forward action in support of goals.

- *Create:* Do all these things, and you will create velocity.

Getting back on course can be this simple—elegant and simple, powerful and simple. But we all get off course sometimes and that does not make us any less amazing—we're like Ferrari sports cars parked in our garages. Not performing because the engine is off. Turn the key and go for a ride.

Are You Off Course? Here Is a Thought about How to Get Back on Track, April 20, 2012

I have been thinking about this topic a lot this week. Partially because I want to ensure that I stay on course with my goals, but also because I see how hard we are on ourselves and the toll this takes on our spirits and desire to keep moving forward. Short-term"itis" perhaps.

I think there is something to be said for believing in ourselves. Really believing. Believing that even though our daily choices are imperfect and our resolve wanes at times . . . and even though we sometimes say one thing and 30 seconds later do the opposite . . . that we are fully capable of massive and transformative progress. That we can do _____ and we can be the one that others think about when searching for a good role model. "Nothing stops her," they will remark.

Few aspects of our lives require perfection to work. This is true! Woo-hoo! Yippee-ki-yay! Momentum, progress, small wins, sweet daily victories, moments of glorious clarity—that's the ticket to success.

Don't let being off course become a source of power pulling you away from your goal. See it for what it is—a speck of time that will be gone in a minute. If in the next minute we become the change we seek, we can skip forward once again and future setbacks will also be insignificant. Keep the progress big and the setbacks minuscule.

Enjoy being in alignment in this moment. And don't look back.

I believe in the main assertion of these posts—that we are amazing, even if we are not doing our best work right now. Do you believe that people have the potential to be great? It is important that you do and that you never give up on your employees (while you also use your accountability practices to establish standards).

Give It a Try!

- Remind your employees that they are *amazing*. Use the word *amazing*. It makes people smile inside. But you have to mean it. Mean it.

- Help them chill out about setbacks and bring some perspective to the discussion.

- Help them do something small that feels like progress. We all love progress.

2. Learn from Them

This post proves that sometimes a short story or quote can make a huge difference. I cannot tell you how many times I have shared this Tony Bennett story, but it always makes people think anew. There is no more powerful way to engage our employees than to have them feel like k.d. lang did in this story.

Hello, My Name Is Tony Bennett...., February 08, 2008

Did you watch *CBS Sunday Morning* last week? We always watch. Love it. If you saw last week's show, you caught the piece they did on k.d. lang. Here is the part that struck me. They were talking about the album k.d. did with Tony Bennett and how it came about. They interviewed Tony Bennett and apparently, Tony had been a big fan of k.d.'s work. They were both backstage at an awards show and Tony walked up to k.d. and said (I am doing this from memory, so it might not be a perfect quote): "Hello, I am Tony Bennett, I am a big fan of your work, and I would love to work with you sometime."

First, this struck me because Tony Bennett does not need to say, "I'm Tony Bennett" backstage at a music awards show where everyone surely knows who he is. What a wonderful and humble approach!

Second, I can only imagine how wonderful k.d. felt to have a legendary crooner walk up to her and tell her he was a fan of her work and that he wanted to work with her.

This got me thinking. Some of you are like Tony Bennett in the workplace—more experienced, perhaps even legendary. When was the last time you humbly walked up to a new talent and told him or her that you admire his or her work and that you would love to work together on a project one day? What would happen if you did?

Can we all show the grace and presence of the great Tony Bennett? Sure! But more important, know that this is a practice that works for all involved. k.d. lang engaged and Tony Bennett engaged. So this way to show managerial love is a win–win.

Give It a Try!

- Actively seek to learn from your employees.

- Ask them for their advice and counsel on a tough problem.

- Ask each team member to teach the team something. Do this regularly so it becomes a way you work together.

3. Help Them Do What They Love Most

This is a very old post but is precious to me because it tells the story of a guy who loved his job even though he had been doing it for decades at the time I saw him. Each and every one of our employees has things about their jobs that they love. The question is, how often do they get to enjoy the best parts of their jobs? Leaders can have a huge impact on how much of the good stuff we get to do (versus the yucky stuff we all put up with as just part of the job).

Shake Your Piano, April 26, 2005

Last week my husband took me to hear David Benoit at Jazz Alley. We got there early and snagged a great table overlooking the stage and slightly behind David. I could see his fingers moving a million miles an hour, using each and every key, even the first one and last one.

It was a great performance that made me smile. Here's the cool part. He was playing so hard that the piano was shaking. I had never seen that before, but he had the big black beast jiving to his beat. David Benoit has been around a while, and he's playing many of the same tunes. Even so, when he plays he is on fire. He was working harder and with more enthusiasm than his three band members combined. These were young guys who should have been playing their hearts out. But it was not their music. Not their legacy. Not their names on the tickets. They were very good, by the way, just not like David. So ownership—extreme ownership—has something to do with it.

As I was watching David shake his piano, I thought about the things I felt that strongly about. Those things I would be willing to "do" for the thousandth time with passion and energy. For me, the list contains serious and silly things:

- Air conducting (I love doing that)

- Coaching a willing person

- Facilitating breakthroughs

- Writing creative nonfiction about a topic with which I am fascinated

- Driving a bit too fast on a beautiful day with the top down or on my motorcycle (cool jazz playing)

- Savoring great chocolate

- Brainstorming new ideas

- Traveling to new places

- Taking on new challenges at work—so foreign that one should wonder if I know how to begin

No job—with a company or my own—will offer these experiences all the time.

No life—regardless of the money I make—will offer these experiences all the time.

Nor does David Benoit's.

Along with the opportunity to play to an eager audience, he has to do PR interviews, spend lots of time on airplanes and in hotels, and I am sure there are other hassles. But it's all for those moments when he can play *his* stuff.

In a way, he ought to enjoy those times, otherwise the crappie hotel beds and endless runway delays wouldn't be worth it. Right?

So what about us? Do we ensure that we experience the great parts—and enjoy them fully—so that it all works out to be a great life? I think many of us (present company included) don't do enough to make sure we are still shakin' the piano.

What's on your list?

I should read this post every week to remind myself to make sure I am experiencing the best parts of my work. If you do the same for yourself and your employees, engagement will soar.

Give It a Try!

- *Ask people what they love most about their jobs.* Then make sure they can do these things often.

- *Use your team members' interests to liven up meetings and the work week.* For example, ask the person who loves TED videos to pick one to share. Ask the person who enjoys mapping complex processes to lead the group in mapping one. Ask the person who enjoys exposure to senior leadership to present at such a gathering on your behalf.

- *Take 15 minutes each week to try something new to bring some fun into the workplace.* Cupcakes are great, but try other things too (not just food), like taking a walk together or spending making everyone use the time to create a new idea.

4. Encourage New Bravery

This post is somewhat embarrassing, but here goes nothing! I selected it because I think that we should all help our employees stretch and experience exciting, nervous, new experiences that require a bit of bravery. It makes us feel more alive.

Remember When We Were Courageous? Seemingly Fearless?
May 14, 2012

I was walking on the treadmill tonight while listening to my iPod. I have a playlist of up-tempo songs great for walking. The song

"Relax" came on from Frankie Goes to Hollywood. I thought about something I did when I was in my early 20s to this song . . . Get your mind out of the gutter . . .

Before I tell you what I did, let me come clean and admit I was a serious disco queen. A total disco freak. I loved it all, especially the somewhat funky stuff like Depeche Mode, the Cure, Eurythmics, and others. I also had a thing for Barry White, but who didn't?

One more thing before I tell you what I did to the song "Relax." Since I am confessing my dorky music tastes and seriously dating myself, let me say that I am a huge fan of Yanni. Yep. Oh, and John Tesh's sports anthems. And Enya. But I also like the Fray, Neon Trees, and My Chemical Romance if that helps. Back to my story of courage.

I lived in Tampa when I was in my early 20s. I was going to college, was a waitress at a TGI Fridays and then a night audit manager at a hotel. I never had any money. I started driving a motorcycle because I couldn't afford a car (or a proper bike, mine was a piece-of-crap Honda 100 with one wobbly wheel). To make extra money, I entered dance contests. They were big in that day.

At first, I entered contests with some guy I met that night and we danced as a couple. Disco was great because, unlike ballroom or some other more coordinated dances, two people could do their own things and look like they were a pair. Dancing in a couple, we won about a third of the time. The total payout was usually $100, or $125 for the better competitions. Not bad!

I remember the first time I entered a dance contest without a guy. Just myself. The discotheque was packed. It was one of the nicer places in town, unlike the ABC Liquor Store bar where I went a lot because it was statistically easier to win the dance contests there (fewer people, drunker clientele). On this night, the place was nice ($150 prize, I think), the crowd was big and looked hip, and I could assume the competition would be tough.

What made me think I could win against several pairs of dancers? What gave me the confidence to dance alone in front of a room full of judging eyes? I still don't know how I might have rationalized entering this contest. I talked myself into it—and, no, I was not drunk—and I entered as a single. I got to pick my song and I selected "Relax" because of its great crescendos and thundering beat. Whenever any DJ put "Relax" on, I always danced to it—I knew every inflection point. I danced my heart out—left it all out on the dance floor—no reservations. I did not win.

After that night, I entered a few more contests on my own, and I won only one (to the unlikely song, "Shock the Monkey" if I recall).

Thinking about it now 25+ years later, I wonder where I got the courage to do it. Was I fearless then? Not at all—I can remember being filled with fear. But courage is not the absence of fear; it is acting in the face of it.

I want to tap into that more courageous Lisa more often. And not just in a life-threatening situation, like a car accident. I want to be courageous and seemingly fearless when I don't need to be—like at the disco. It feels wowy, tingly. It's like ice cream *and* the head freeze. The pain and pleasure of New Mexican green chilies. Lovely and overwhelming. I know the courageous Lisa is down in there somewhere.

I bet you have your own story of the more courageous you. Reflect on that time and enjoy it again. Who were you being that you did that? What's going on in your life today that could use that *you*?

Food for thought. Now go shake it.

Do you still respect me even though I like Yanni? How might you show your bravery? If you go first, your employees will more likely follow.

Give It a Try!

- Ask your employees what's on their bucket/career goal list that they are a bit frightened of? Help them explore this idea.

- Ask them to do things that require a bit of bravery, like making a big presentation or researching alternatives from other industries, or talking on a new aspect of their role (like a project leader). And *then* (very important), be there to help them succeed. You don't just want to toss them in the deep end without water wings.

- Delight in sharing moments of bravery. It will set a tone for more to follow.

5. Help Them Create an Exciting New Goal

This type of managerial love is particularly important for our high performers because we probably are not challenging them as much as they would like (and perhaps not enough to keep them engaged and employed!). I am a fairly assertive person, and so I tend to manage up and help my manager do this for me. It would be even better if my manager came to me and encouraged it (or better yet, expected it).

The Animated You, May 07, 2010

How are you doing? How are you feeling? Are you jazzed about something? Is there something compelling you to move forward? I have a friend I will call Jerry. Jerry is an amazing leader who occasionally gets in a funk—in a rut—in a blah space. It is not depression, not a lack of imagination or commitment. He gets comfortable with the status quo. Do you know a Jerry? We need to shake things up every now and then. Do something different. Strike out and challenge ourselves in a big way.

OK, this post is not about Jerry, it is about me (although Jerry is a real person). Last week I was thinking about life and realized that I have gotten excessively automatic. I don't have a big goal now—nothing on the horizon that represents a significant challenge. This is incredible because I always have big goals. Always. Books, motorcycle tours, nonprofit projects, degrees, geographic moves—something. This should have been obvious to me, but I will tell you it was not. I said to myself, I don't have a big goal.... I don't have a big goal.... how is this possible? I have plenty of smaller goals, but nothing significant. The realization hit me like a knock on the head.

The absence of a big goal impacts how well we achieve our small goals, too. It affects how we approach our work and the overall vibe we feel and share. Our management practices tell the story of who we are. My habits and practices tell the story of who I am. This is the way it is for all of us. What story are your actions telling? Do you like this story? Does it excite you? If you, like me, are in a bit of a stall/rut/slowdown/coast/pause, what should you do? Here is the formula:

1. *Create a goal.* Pick a goal that makes the hairs on the back of your neck tingle when you tell people about it. A goal that is compelling enough to make you uncomfortable.

2. *Share your goal.* Get out there and talk, talk, talk. Share your goal in a way that expresses what it is, why it is important to you, and the difference it will make when you get there.

3. *Align your context.* Change something—or many somethings—to rearrange your reality to nudge you on the path toward your new goal. Change something!

4. *Take small daily actions that are aligned with your goal.* Tiny actions every day create momentum and are much better than being a weekend warrior.

5. *Enroll others.* Make big requests that move your goal forward.

And this is how we become the animated versions of ourselves. Animated means being visibly full of life. It starts with step 1—the neck-tingling goal and source of excitement and drive. Something that inspires you, moves you, changes your perspective. Something that is worth taking a stand for. What's mine? I am working on defining it right now.....If you need some inspiration, check out my previous posts about goal setting. I'm enjoying reading them and getting ideas about my big goal. Here are a few of the questions I am asking myself:

- What's something I have always wanted to do, but haven't?

- If money and time were not barriers, what would I do?

- What am I too scared to do?

- What type of activities make me happy and bring out the "animated" me?

- How can I use my strengths to benefit others?

- Who would I most like to partner with?

- If I were told I had only a short time to live, how would I choose to spend my time?

- What's the wildest idea I can think of?

How might you answer these questions? I'll share my goal when I know what it is.

Interesting story about my real friend Jerry. He had been in the same role for a long time with different organizations and had not stretched himself to go to that next level. He was operating in third gear but was a six-gear sports car! Finally, he decided to lead more fully and he went for a higher role and was very successful. He was actually promoted again within six months and his leadership blossomed. We can do this for ourselves, and we can help others grow and get beyond routine ruts.

Give It a Try!

- Talk about the types of things listed in the post at your one-on-ones. Reserve time to inquire and listen (not just 5 minutes at the end; try 30 minutes at a minimum).

- Recognize when employees are stuck in third gear and take the initiative to offer a positive way to get reengaged.

- Get to know your team members' BIG goals or hopes and do what you can to contribute to their progress. Showing an interest and discussing it (you doing most of the listening) means a lot to people.

6. and 7. Listen Deeply, and Be a "Yes" Person

Ways 6 and 7 to show managerial love are discussed together here because that is the way the blog post was written. It contains two distinct tips, and I love them both so I combined them. Check out the entire post and then I will address each tip separately. This is one of my favorite posts, and these practices are powerful and electrifying. Promise!

Helping Others Zoom Forward: Two Ways, August 12, 2010

I am working on a 30-minute keynote about breakthroughs where I will spend the last 10 minutes focusing on how we can catalyze breakthroughs for others. The first 20 minutes will make the case why small daily actions are our most powerful tools for generating breakthroughs (chaos/butterfly effect, brain chemistry/plasticity, going beyond SMART goals/importance of progress, Dale Carnegie on steroids/inviting a challenge).

Here are my talking points for the second part. Tell me what you think!

Catalyzing Breakthroughs

There are few things as satisfying and meaningful than when we can help catalyze breakthroughs. We have the opportunity to extend our impact, reach, and legacy well beyond what we can do ourselves. Keeping in mind our breakthrough principles, I'd like to share two practices that can be highly *catalytic*.

But first, let's define the term *catalyst*. A catalyst is a substance that increases the rate of a chemical reaction but is not consumed in the process. In everyday terms, a catalyst is something that makes a result easier to achieve. Imagine you wanted to take supplies from the top of one mountain to another, and there was a deep and narrow valley in between. You could build a road down the side of one mountain and up the other and that might make it easier to go fast. Or you could build a bridge across the valley and make it even easier to get the supplies across. The bridge is the catalyst. It makes something easier and is not consumed by the process.

How can we make it easier for people to be more focused and in action? How can we help catalyze breakthroughs? Here are two of my favorite ways.

The Sponge Stance

A couple of years ago, I did twenty-five back-to-back training classes in a large office building in downtown Seattle. Each morning, I would enjoy a latte in the lobby Starbucks. These early moments were peaceful and reflective. I watched people line up for their caffeine fixes and sit at the small, round tables with colleagues and friends. I observed a broad spectrum of listening styles and was most fascinated by the people who seemed completely engrossed in what the other person was saying. This observation was the inspiration for what I now call the sponge stance.

Imagine that you went down to your favorite coffee shop for a mid-day infusion of caffeine. You are standing in line and you notice that the person standing in front of you is someone you admire a great deal—someone famous, a great leader, author, innovator, or historical figure. You summon the courage to introduce yourself to this person and ask her if she would like to have a coffee and chat with you. She agrees. Now imagine that you are sitting across from her at one of those small, round café tables. She is talking, and you are hanging on every word she is saying. Your eyes are fixed on her face, and you are unaware of what's going on beyond your conversation. You think she is amazing, and you are enjoying taking in each word, inflection, and nonverbal cue. You are like a sponge, fully soaking up her messages.

What do you think it feels like to be listened to in this way? Have you been listened to like this? What if, not every time, but sometimes, you listened to your employees, peers, or friends in this way? What might be possible? Our best thinking doesn't usually plop out of our mouths right away. We need to noodle and play with the topic, and this takes time. Do we give others the time and absolute attention they need?

This is the sponge stance—the way we listen when we demonstrate a complete interest in and focus on the other person. It's the way we listen when we think the other person is amazing—when we admire who she is and what she is doing. In the years that I have been telling people about the sponge stance, several have asked if what I am describing is the same thing as active listening (which means not interrupting, asking for clarification, not thinking about what you are going to say, parroting back what you hear, paying attention, empathizing, minimizing distractions, and reflecting on and synthesizing the information). I don't think the two approaches are the same—nor are they in conflict with one another. The sponge stance is listening that demonstrates our regard for the performer and our admiration for what she is trying to accomplish. Do you really hear what others are saying? If we want to help make big things happen, we need to listen deeply and well.

Make Reverse Requests

I am a fan of making requests to generate breakthroughs. If we do not ask, how will the people who care about us know what we need? Here's a different twist on how to use the power of a request—I call it the reverse request to catalyze breakthroughs.

I first discovered the power of a reverse request by accident. My husband Bill and I were traveling and I was making conversation— small talk—throwing out seemingly meaningless questions for the fun of it. But then I hit upon a question that changed our lives forever. The question was "If you could live anywhere, doing any kind of work, where would you live and what would you do?" Seems simple enough, right? To my surprise, Bill said that he would like to live in Seattle and have his own geology consulting business. We lived in New Mexico at the time, and he had never mentioned Seattle or starting a business. This is something I did not know and might never have known because he is the type of guy who does not advocate on his own behalf very often. I had not been to Seattle, knew little about it but said, "Well, why don't we do that?" I got a job with Amazon.com, and six weeks later we were living in Seattle and my husband had started his own consulting firm. Eleven years later, he is still enjoying his work at his company, Haneberg Geoscience. I often wonder what our lives be like if I had not asked this one question. I was just making conversation and was not trying to change the course of things. Do you know your spouse's dreams? Really?

A reverse request happens when you help others make requests. Here are a few examples of reverse requests:

- You know what someone wants, and so you go ahead and offer it (or some version of it), sparing him or her the difficult task of asking for it.

- You engage in a conversation that helps someone articulate what she wants. Then you ask what you or someone else could do that would be most helpful.

- You provide the courage—courage on loan—that helps someone else make something big happen.

I have a friend who is very conservative when it comes to being assertive about her hopes, dreams, and wishes. She does not want to be a bother, and so she feels a bit selfish asking about these things closest to her heart (I am not putting words in her mouth; we have talked about this). But it's not selfish to make requests, because when we are at our best, everyone wins. Yet because this is a struggle for my friend, she generally does not get around to sharing her requests. Sometimes I put myself in her shoes and share with her what I think she would ask for if she had the courage. So far, I have been right every time. When I offer her help, she says "yes," and things surge forward for her. I would bet that you have a friend or coworker like this, too.

Reverse requests are a great way to help catalyze breakthroughs. Be a "Yes" Person!

Give It a Try! Assume the Sponge Stance (Listen Deeply)

I often end courses with the story of the sponge stance because it punctuates an important point for all leaders—we can make a big difference in the lives of others if we listen deeply and inspire their best. Now you try it:

- Assume the sponge stance with one person each day and eventually do this with all team members.

- Remind yourself of your team member's best qualities before you meet with him or her. Doing so will show up in your listening.

- Practice MBWA (managing by walking around) every day. Don't have a set agenda—that would not be MBWA, that would be updating, which is not usually engaging. Have no set purpose except to touch base.

Give It a Try! Make Reverse Requests

I love the reverse request technique and have used it many times. There may be no more immediate way to help your employees progress than to make reverse requests. But be forewarned, you should not do this for people who do not need it because it can feel pushy and over-managing even if you are trying to help! Now you try it:

- Get to know your team members—what are their goals and big dreams? Ask them what they would do if time and resources were not a barrier. Suggest, "Why not do it?"

- Ask, "Would it help or make a difference if you had _____?" If he or she says "yes," be ready to help make it happen.

- Be the bearer of nice surprises every now and then like asking if Sally would like to attend a course because there is some budget money available.

8. Blast Away Hassles That Distract Them

This is an odd blog post, I will admit, but it illustrates the tip very well. As a leader, one of the best gifts we can give our employees is a workplace that has less hassle and more meaning. If your employees go home at the end of the day feeling defeated by endless meetings and emails, then they will have neither the energy nor the desire to engage.

The Creative Space—Real Space and the Space in Your Head, June 27, 2008

I have been thinking about the act of creation. Or should I say re-creation, since everything springs forth from something else. The dilemma we have is that we need to unplug to create. Some of you might argue with this point and say that you can create while the email ping sounds, your cell phone vibrates with a new text, and you overhear ten different cubicle conversations. I would argue that you could be creating at a much deeper level if you focused more effectively.

Note: My email just pinged. I went to look, deleted the new message, and now I am back. It is taking me a few moments to get back into what I was writing for this post.

. . . We need to unplug to create. I know this to be true for my writing. The best writing comes when I shut down all outside influences for at least four hours. This is tough with all the plugged-in things we have in our lives and the people and pets who seek our attention.

And then there are bodily functions and thirst and temperature and other physical interruptions that pop up.

Note: My writing was just halted by thoughts of being cold. I could not decide whether or not to turn the heat on because it will be hot later and so may be best to keep the room cold and put on a fleece pullover. Or perhaps I should get on the water rower and generate heat.

Creation demands our undivided attention. And yet, so many of us find this a hard gift to give ourselves. Even the little red squiggly line that pops under misspelled words can disrupt thinking.

Note: Another ping. Should I look? Heck, I have already diverted my attention, might as well look. Two messages, deleted them both. Where was I?

Perhaps instead of a sensory deprivation tank, we need a disruption-free module in our backyards. We could remodel an Airstream Bambi and make it a safe zone. Or get one of those new office sheds. But the key would be to not bring cell phones, email, phones, or other potential distracters into the module.

Note: Another ping. It's OK, I am still distracted, because I am still cold and have not put on another layer. This email is good—the REI summer sale starts today.

When I think about great writers—Hemingway, Steinbeck, and other dead guys—I imagine they went to secluded places where they could write undisturbed. I have been to Hemingway's home in Key West and, other than the genetically mutated extra-toed cats, it seems like a place that would have allowed him to focus while writing.

Note: I am now distracted by my own mental interruption. I can't help but wonder why there are both too many wild chickens and too many street cats in Key West. It seems as though one would take care of the other and they would just have too many freak fat cats. Having an extra toe means having an extra claw, too. One more weapon against the chickens. But this has nothing to do with creativity.

Note: The heater just kicked on, which tells me that I was not being a sissy, it was cold in here (we have the thermostat set at 67, so it must be colder than this).

I am trying to think back to the last time I was able to create in a . . . .

Note: Another ping. Looked. It's my daily Publisher's Lunch email.

I am trying to think back to the last time I was able to shut out the disruptions to create. It has been a long time. I have read about famous writers who said that they took years to write a book. I always marveled at this because it seems like such a long time. But maybe this is because it takes that long to string together bits of uninterrupted writing time.

An hour here.

Twenty-five minutes there.

Two hours last week.

Etcetera.

Note: I am distracted by the fact that this is likely the first time I have ever typed out the word etcetera in a sentence. It looks strange. We get so used to abbreviations.

Note: The heater is still going, which tells me that it was very cold in my office. No wonder I was having a hard time thinking.

What is the solution to this conundrum? How can we possibly create within the mess that is our everyday lives? I think we need to do the best we can to reduce distractions. Turn the ping off, the cell phone off, go to the bathroom, dress comfortably, go for a pre-thinking walk, pet the cats, fill up a large mug of coffee, and try to create.

I am giggling reading this post again. It is such a real illustration of what happens! It's funny, but it is also tragic because, regardless what we all might like to think, we cannot multitask, and every interruption sets our progress back. Peace and less hassle are great gifts to give our team members.

Give It a Try!

- Create "no interruption zones" in the department that team members can use when they need to focus.

- Encourage people to take care of their needs and use tools and practices that enable them to reduce distractions.

- Establish regular times during the week for planning and innovation (and other more proactive stuff).

9. Put More BANG! and WOW! into Meetings

Oh, my, this is such a fun idea! I hope you give it a try. There is some overlap between this way to show managerial love and the expansion conversation described in the previous chapter, but it is worth discussing in both chapters because the practice is simple and highly underutilized.

Do Their Minds BANG! WOW! Or Do They Leave with a Whimper and Sigh? April 02, 2012

I was thinking about a course I attended a few months ago. The facilitator asked me for feedback. It was a good course and offered solid information. The facilitator did a fine job, and the participants seemed satisfied. Good. Solid. Fine. Satisfied.

I told her that I thought she missed two opportunities. First, the course was not designed to deliver any aha moments—the potential for a mind-blowing epiphany was zero. A wise man once asked me, challenged me, what my big idea was for a book project I was proposing. I had no big idea. This course offered no big ideas. Miss.

The second miss was that the course started slow, warmed to medium, and ended medium. There was no narrative arc. Courses can benefit from using the principles of story construction. The flow helps you manage and generate energy. This course was perfectly fine but draining. All whimper, no bang. Miss.

And what about your next staff meeting. Ah! Gotcha! You thought I was talking about a training class, and since you don't lead training classes that I was not talking to you—right? Well consider this. I see the same two misses in meetings. That they offer no big ideas— there is no or only low potential of an aha moment. And they are not designed to generate and retain energy. Miss. Miss.

Don't have another meeting until you think about this. Even if you have a meeting coming up in two hours, you can do something to make it better. Bring in a big idea. Share something that has the potential to make people think anew. You might fail, but no problem, try again next week. No attempt = no potential. It breaks my heart.

The facilitator, who is a friend, felt frustrated and devastated, I could tell. She had done a good job but had let habit shroud her determination as a teacher and catalyst. I am glad she was devastated because she is talented, special, and can do better. She needed the dissonance to reconnect with why she teaches. Whenever we get people together, we need to strive for better.

This post highlights a cautionary tale about missed opportunities. I think it is easy to add more interest and excitement into conversations with just a little bit of forethought and planning. Remember that my definition of managerial love is taking initiative—and that's all we need to do to make average gatherings more engaging.

Give It a Try!

- Invite interesting guest speakers to your meetings.

- Ask team members for ideas and then let them help.

- Carve out time for learning at every staff meeting and ask your training department for ideas (or to help!).

10. Be Interested in Them

Although I have this post and idea listed last, don't interpret that I think it is less important or useful. On the contrary, this way to show managerial love is fundamental and should be at the core of your leadership practices. As you will read in the post, this way of being does not come naturally to everyone (not for me at least!), but we can all work toward being someone who makes people feel cared for and great.

I Saw the Master in Action This Weekend, January 22, 2012

I spent an afternoon with a dear friend yesterday. We chatted over lunch and walked around his beach town. I have always admired his engaging and caring way—he is a leader who makes others feel like they have his full attention and consideration, and they do (that's the important part—it is sincere, not an act). Why? Because he thinks and lives this way. He notices people and things and takes the initiative to be helpful and caring. More so than most people. More so than I do—by a long shot.

I have always known this about my friend, but I was reminded—in a vivid way—during our walk. Those who we passed received a smile and hello. Someone had dropped a baby bottle on the walking path, he picked it up and put it on the cement wall so the owner could find it and no one would trip over it. We passed a couple who were taking pictures of each other, and he asked if he could take their picture together and then had some fun with them to make sure they got a great shot. He interacted with people on the street, in shops, and in the restaurant in ways that made each smile and brighten.

You might be thinking that I am a little nuts for calling this out because these human acts are quite normal—or they should be. It is true that any one of these moments would be considered what it means to be a good person—nothing extraordinary.

But here is the distinction. He oozed care in every moment. He was aware of others, noticed others, proactively cared for others, and did so while being fully engaged in our conversation. I was much less aware of others.

My friend is someone for whom people love working, and he brings out the best in them. And here is the main point of this post. We can and should do this too. It does not take a training class or being a particular behavioral style. We can relate to others in this way if we

- Choose to be a powerful and positive influence on others.

- Take the time and attention to notice others.

- Be gracious, kind, friendly, and helpful more often.

Don't go rushing to include these expectations in your new employee orientation. Don't add it to your performance review or create a management competency called "caring." Just try being more demonstrably caring and see what happens. Lead from a basis of positive care for others, and you will find that your days, weeks, and years are more amazing and that your good vibe spreads.

After spending the afternoon with my friend, I found myself thinking about how I can improve what I notice and how I respond to others. I am no ogre, by the way, but I can and want to demonstrate care more often—for everyone, not just a chosen few.

You have likely heard the mind teaser about the tree—if a tree falls in a forest but no one is there to hear it, does it make a sound?

I have to ask the same thing about caring for others. If we care, but no one experiences our affection and goodwill, does it exist? I think that the vast majority of people are caring in terms of intentions. Most of us, however, are quite selective about how we give of ourselves. I am not sure this serves us, our intentions, or others well.

These tiny actions—smiles, pictures, gestures of help—add up to make a very big and wonderful impression. Remember that although this benefit is compelling, it should not be the reason that we choose to live a more generous (of ourselves) life. My friend does not think about this. In fact, I am guessing he would think this blog post is quite odd indeed.

Each of our employees needs and deserves a little bit of our undivided attention. I have seen how showing an interest affects others, and it takes no more time than ignoring people. The story in the post was real—we both took the same walk that took the same amount of time. He brought smiles to several people's faces; I did not. That was an opportunity lost.

Give It a Try!

- Always acknowledge people with a smile.

- I had one manufacturing client that used the old-fashioned handshake as a daily greeting for all employees. They loved it.

- Set a goal to spontaneously help at least one person per day. I realize that planning to do something spontaneously seems odd, but it works. Just don't manufacture the opportunity to check it off the list.

Conclusion

I hope you are gushing with ideas on how to show more love. Even though I wrote these posts, I learn more each time I revisit them. You will be most effective when you share your brand of managerial love (based on your style and strengths). Our best will energize and inspire. Promise! In the next chapter, we will explore ways to bring your intentions together into an effective work regimen.

CHAPTER SIXTEEN

Using Design Principles to Balance and Optimize Accountability and Engagement

When I think about how leaders can use design principles, I get the image of a bento. I have always loved bento box meals because they have lots of wonderful things within them and they feel complete. The origin of the bento is Japanese, but you see versions of the bento box in many cuisines. Here is a delicious looking bento (Figure 16.1).

Figure 16.1. A Japanese Bento Box

Am I making you hungry yet? I like the metaphor of the bento box because it illustrates the type of design principles we need to use to cultivate highly accountable and engaged teams. The trick is getting all the good practices into our jam-packed days and creating the environment that builds a productive culture.

The 11 secrets and the other tools and ideas presented in Section II have given you a flavor of the types of practices that will produce the best results for you. And I have no doubt that you want to use your precious time (Secret 10!) well and for the greatest benefit. After all, we need to also take care of our own engagement.

Secret 11 suggests that design is the secret to performance velocity because you will need to be deliberate about how you craft your leadership regimens and design your workplace to be successful. Let's look at two design ideas through the bento box metaphor.

Your Leadership Bento Box

When we design something, we define and structure it based on the impact we want it to have, and we can and should do this for how we spend time. The elements that go into your leadership bento box might include the following:

- Planning
- Meetings
- Team time
- MBWA
- Social time

- Advocacy time
- Innovation
- Performance discussions
- Partnering

Here's a graphic for how that might look (Figure 16.2).

Figure 16.2. Your Leadership Bento Box

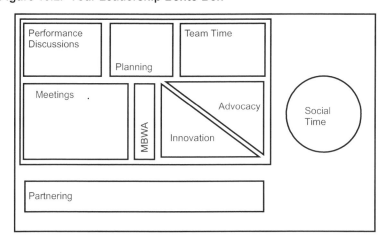

Think of the large rectangle in the diagram is your 40-hour work week (or 20 hours if you are a working manager who leads part time). Each leadership practice has a place and is important (just like the ginger and the must-have wasabi next to the sushi roll). When we take the time to decide with great forethought how we will spend our time, we will more likely get to the good stuff. I say "more likely" because we all know that stuff happens, and our schedules get hijacked by issues that need to be addressed. This is the nature of leadership but that does not mean we should not do what we can to create the best possible structure for our work.

Here are some of the best practices I have seen that help with establishing and sticking to the desired design for how leaders spend their time:

- Schedule regular meetings well in advance (monthly one-on-ones, team gatherings, networking time).

- Block off time every day to MBWA and for informal conversations.

- Block off time every day that can be used for planning and for proactive work.

- Plan regular sessions for team innovation. Make it a habit, not an exception.

- Put birthdays, anniversaries, and other major days on your calendar so you never forget.

- Structure team meetings to have standing agenda items for learning, feedback, and fun.

- Talk about the things that are important and encourage the entire team to spend time wisely.

- Say "no" to meetings that are not a good use of your time.

- Do not invite people to meetings if attending is not a good use of their time.

- Decide on email etiquette standards and communicate them broadly (no "reply all" unless critical, no "bcc," use email lists sparingly, craft better subject lines, and so on).

You might think I am being unrealistic with the above suggestion that you say "no" to more meetings, but I am not. I know that sometimes we cannot control our time, but I think we have more control than we use. I was once an interim product development director for a company—a role in which lots of people struggled and failed. The plan was that I would take the role for a short period of time and use my magical organization development skills to analyze the issues and help redesign the role for success. We would then recruit and hire someone to fill the newly aligned role. It was a fun assignment, and I instantly honed in on one of the key issues. Meetings! Because the person in the role was the overall product development leader, he or she ended up getting invited to *every* meeting about every aspect of *all* products. This was a long-standing practice and meant that whoever was in the role already had over 35 hours of meetings a week before making any decisions of their own about what needed to get done.

I did not know which meetings were critical and which were not, so I decided to not go to any and see what would happen. Before you think that I was an inconsiderate meanie, I should tell you that I sent all the affected parties an email saying that I would not be able to attend the meeting but would be available on "stand by" in case they needed me. I did not want to hold anyone up, but I also know that I did not have the time for all these standing meetings.

Here's how my experiment went. (I am not making this up, by the way, it really happened.) In over half the cases, I was never called and no work was slowed down. A third of the meetings needed me some of the time and being on call worked for them. Only about six hours of meetings had to be added back into my schedule because it was very clear that I was a critical participant. One of my peers came into my office and said, "Lisa, you are not going to any meetings!" I replied, "Yes, isn't it wonderful, I recommend you do the same thing!" I also encouraged my team to look at their schedules and make adjustments where it made sense. There were even a few meetings that stopped entirely, which was a nice gift for everyone involved.

Meetings in themselves are not the problem because we get important things done at them. The problem is that we tend to invite too many people to our meetings, and when we are invited to meetings, we tend to accept too much of the time. If time were money and we had to pay people's salaries when they met with us, this would not happen. But because it is all fuzzy money, we spend time like it is a two-penny gumball.

I don't want to harp too much about meetings because this is just one element of our leadership bento box (albeit, one with which many leaders struggle). Applying design to your work means being more intentional about how you spend your time. I cannot give you a formula or a template because you each need to create your own bento box. If you know you need to spend more time on the engagement side, your bento should reflect this. If you are not consistent enough with your accountability practices (true for most leaders), then accountability practices should be more fully designed into your schedule.

Your Workplace Bento Box

Your Leadership Bento Box guides you to use design to structure your leadership practices and schedule. You can and should also use design to create a workplace that supports accountability and inspires engagement. The Workplace Bento Box has some different elements:

- Physical appearance
- Gathering spaces
- Values and norms
- Social time
- Team time

- Events

- Meaning of the work

- Pace and rate of change

- Partnering

Here's a graphic for how that might look (see Figure 16.3).

Figure 16.3 Your Workplace Bento Box

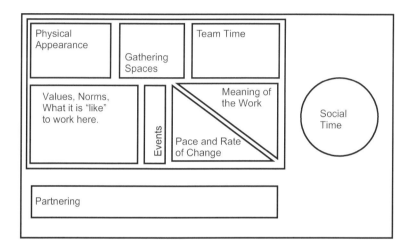

OK, it is the same graphic as before with different words, but you get the idea. Design means being intentional about what you want to see. This applies to the workplace and is very important for both accountability and engagement. Take an inventory of how each of these elements are either helping or hindering performance velocity. Do you want team members to collaborate more but offer no space for them to get together? Do you want the workplace to be fun and exciting, but all you see are gray walls and boring beige carpet? Would a fly on the wall (if it were very smart) guess what's most important if it hung around your department for a week?

For those of you who are middle managers (and not the top boss), I can imagine that you might feel somewhat limited in what you can do to design the workplace. In some respects this is true—you might not be able to paint or buy art. But remember the story about Tim the human fire hose and his under-performing team (chapter 5)? He was a middle manager for a company that was very cheap, and he still managed to change the entire look and feel of

If you want something, you need to design for it.

the workplace with his consistent efforts to show his team managerial love. It's hard, but it can be done. That's why we got into this line of work, right?

For example, let's say you want to create a more high energy and collaborative team vibe because you think that this change would benefit both the team members and the organization. Sounds reasonable—nearly every one of my clients is looking to do this. When my clients share their frustrations over lack of progress toward this goal, I ask a pretty standard set of questions:

- What are your collaboration practices? When do team members spend time collaborating?

- How many teaming permutations do you use to get things done (whole team, duos, triads, small groups, task committees, and so on)?

- If I were to walk around the office (and intranet), what would I see related to collaboration?

- How often do you and your peers get together to partner and collaborate?

- What type of business problems do you solve through collaboration?

See where I am going with this? When I ask these questions, I always (I don't use the word *always* a lot, but it applies this time) get a deer-in-the-headlights response. *What? I gotta do those things? Dang!* I get it that doing all this is tough, and I don't want to seem like I am beating up on well-intentioned, hard-working leaders. My point is that if you want something, you need to design for it.

As is the case with the Leadership Bento Box, I cannot offer you a specific formula or to-do list to create the optimal workplace. All I can do is offer a few examples and encourage you to be more intentional.

Intentional.

Intentional.

That's what design is all about.

Telling and Using the Secrets

Thanks for joining me on this exploration of the 11 secrets for cultivating highly accountable and engaging teams! I hope that you have found the book helpful, provocative, and a great use of your precious time. It's important to me that you feel this way; I wrote this book because I believed it could be a game changer for many leaders.

To quickly summarize our journey, it is helpful to reference the Accountability and Engagement Model (Figure 12.1) that I shared at the end of Section I—but with one additional element.

Accountability/Engagement and Our Leadership Approach

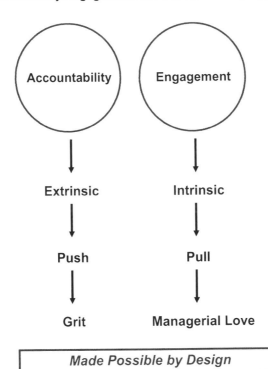

Accountability and engagement are two distinct systems supported by different leadership practices. It is important to know that they are not at all the same, and it is equally important to understand how they impact each other and are connected.

Accountability is a management system; leaders hold people accountable. Accountability practices are extrinsically motivating, and accountability is therefore a push system. The secret to success for any push system is consistency or grit. If you are dissatisfied with the level of accountability in your department, you will want to shore up your leadership practices and ensure that you are clear and consistent and that your expectations conversations are thorough. Accountability is an important part of running a thriving business, but don't rely upon it to produce excellence because it isn't designed to produce this level of performance.

To reach excellence, you need highly engaged team members. Engagement is also a management system but not one that we control (ironic but true!). Employees choose to engage, and engagement is a gift. Leaders can create a work environment that is more engaging, and when they do so, they help ignite their team members' intrinsic motivation. Systems that rely on intrinsic motivation work best when employees pull into their work. We cannot push for, require, or demand engagement. Because engagement is a pull system, the secret to success is managerial love. Managerial love looks like taking initiative on other person's behalf. It's this demonstration of proactive care that creates the pull. We all want to be loved, even by our bosses!

To balance these differing performance needs and systems along with other leadership demands, we need to use design. Design means being deliberate and thoughtful about how we spend time and how we create our workplace culture so that we increase performance velocity (speed of progress and focus on goals). It requires that we make good choices and lead by those choices every day. Organizations often use phrases such as "bake it into the plan," "hardwire it," or "socialize it," and all of these are saying the same thing—design it and make it so. As leaders, this is both our challenge and our opportunity. Leadership is a privilege, but it is also the hardest job we will ever love.

Share the Secrets

I hope you will share these 11 secrets and all the practical tips in the book that are designed to enable you to increase performance velocity. Share the book, check out my website at www.lisahaneberg.com, and engage other leaders in lively discussions about what these secrets mean to you.

I would also encourage you to share the secrets and this book with your team members. There is nothing here that I would not feel comfortable sharing—nothing. In fact, I think it would be in alignment with the secrets to do just that. Our employees expect us to hold them accountable, so let's talk to them about the best ways to do that so we can spend more time and energy on the inspiring stuff of engagement. It's win–win to be open, clear, and inclusive. Our team members are amazing and can help us lead better.

I wish you the best!

Here's to your success using the secrets and honing your leadership practices (imagine I am holding a golden margarita and toasting to your success)! I would love to hear your feedback, so feel free to contact me at lhaneberg@gmail.com. Tell me your story! Who knows, you might end up being "Denny" or "Tim" or "Janice" in some future book (kidding…well, not really). But more important, I would love to know how you are doing, what's working for you, and where you still struggle. That's how I learn and how we all learn.

The 11 secrets for cultivating highly accountable and engaged teams have served me well, and I have seen how they have helped many leaders just like you bring out the best in others. May they bring you, your team, your organization—double the accountability, double the engagement, double the love.

Recommended Reading

Here are some of the books I have mentioned in this book and others that I think can help leaders use the secrets to increase accountability and engagement.

Amabile, Teresa, & Steven J. Kramer. 2010. What Really Motivates Workers. *Harvard Business Review* (January/February).

Block, Peter. 2013. *Stewardship: Choosing Service Over Self-Interest.* San Francisco, CA: Berrett-Koehler.

Bryan, Mark. 1995. *The Artist's Way at Work: Riding the Dragon.* New York: William Morrow.

Csikszentmihalyi, Mihali. 1975. *Beyond Boredom and Anxiety: Experiencing Flow in Work and Play.* San Francisco: Jossey-Bass.

Duarte, Nancy. 2010. *Resonate: Present Visual Stories That Transform Audiences.* Hoboken, NJ: Wiley.

Farber, Steve. 2011. *The Radical Leap Re-energized: Doing What You Love in the Service of People Who Love What You Do.* Tempe, AZ: No Limit Publishing.

Gladwell, Malcolm. 2008. *Outliers: The Story of Success.* New York: Little Brown.

Kohn, Alfie. 1986. *No Contest: The Case Against Competition.* New York: Houghton Mifflin.

———. 1999. *Punished by Rewards: The Trouble with Gold Stars, Incentive Plans, A's, Praise, and Other Bribes.* New York: Houghton Mifflin.

Lencioni, Patrick. 2004. *Death By Meeting: A Leadership Fable About Solving the Most Painful Problem in Business.* San Francisco: Jossey-Bass.

Pink, Daniel. 2006. *A Whole New Mind.* New York: Riverhead Books.

———. 2011. *Drive: the Surprising Truth About What Motivates Us.* New York: Riverhead Books.

Robinson, Ken. 2009. *The Element: How Finding Your Passion Changes Everything.* New York: Penguin Press.

Whitney, Diana, & Amanda Trosten-Bloom. 2003. *The Power of Appreciative Inquiry: A Practical Guide to Positive Change.* San Francisco: Berrett-Koehler.

Zander, Rosamund Stone, & Benjamin Zander. 2000. *The Art of Possibility.* Cambridge, MA: Harvard Business School Press.

Acknowledgements

This book is story driven, and I am thankful to all the great leaders I have worked with and learned from. I am grateful for the lessons learned from less effective leaders too! This particular book could not have been possible without all my readers, clients, and colleagues who helped me hone my ideas and refine the secrets. You told me what resonated and offered your best-kept secrets for success.

I was very lucky that a group of talented leaders and educators gave me some of their precious time to review early drafts of the book. What a wonderful gift, and I appreciate it! I thank you for your interest in my work and your contribution to making this a better book. Elaine Carr, Paul D'Souza, Phil Gerbyshak, Tim Goodheart, CV Harquail, Patricia Hatch, Jackie Jordan-Davis, Peter Levy, Lloyd Lopez, Keith McMahen, Martin Moll, Karen Montijo, Collin Quiring, Beth Rashleigh, Daniel Rera, Curt Rosengren, Ramesh Sehgal, Rajesh Setty, Terry Starbucker, Tanmay Vora, Sharon Walling, Steve Wilson, Tony Wright, and David Zinger—you are the best!

Thanks to my publishing partners at Trainers Publishing House including Cat, Jacki, Nancy, and Dawn, who I have worked with on several other writing projects. It is fun when you get to work with people you know, trust, and love. You have made this project a joy, and I am very proud of the product we produced!

Thank you to my husband, Bill, who has supported my work (and my loony ways) for fifteen years. It is nice to know you have my back when I need to set all things aside to meet deadlines.

About the Author

Lisa Haneberg is an organization development, leadership, and management author, trainer, researcher, practitioner, and consultant. She has over 25 years of experience providing executive and management development and training and coaching solutions for large and small organizations (including health care, manufacturing, services, nonprofit, and government organizations). She has particular expertise in the areas of senior team development, performance management, executive coaching, talent management, succession planning, organizational agility and alignment, and middle management effectiveness.

Lisa's other book titles include

- *Organization Development Basics* (ASTD Press)

- *Coaching Basics* (ASTD Press)

- *Focus Like a Laser Beam: 10 Ways to Do What Matters Most* (Jossey-Bass)

- *Two Weeks to a Breakthrough: How to Zoom Toward Your Goal in 14 Days or Less* (Jossey-Bass)

- *10 Steps to Be a Successful Manager* (ASTD Press)

- *Developing Great Managers: 20 Power Hours* (ASTD Press)

- *Hip and Sage: Staying Smart, Cool, and Competitive in the Workplace* (Davies-Black)

- *The High Impact Middle Manager: Powerful Strategies to Thrive in the Middle* (ASTD Press)

- *High Impact Middle Management: Solutions for Today's Busy Public-Sector Managers* (ASTD Press)

- *Coaching Up and Down the Generations* (ASTD Press & Berrett-Koehler)

- *Connecting Top Managers: Developing Executive Teams for Business Success* (Co-author with James Taylor, Financial Times Press)

- *The Management Development Handbook* (Editor, ASTD Press)

- *Never Ending New Beginnings* (A self-published "Best of Management Craft" book)

In addition, her work has been highlighted in publications such as *Leader to Leader, Washington CEO, Capital*, and *Leadership Excellence*. Lisa is a nationally recognized thought leader and speaker. In 2011, she won the HCI M-Prize for management innovation (a competition judged by management legend Gary Hamel). Lisa has held both internal and external consulting roles in organizations such as Memorial Hermann Health System, Amazon.com, Intel, MedCentral, Black & Decker, Mead Paper, Corbis, Promedica, MTD Products, Perfetti vanMelle, TUI Travel International, Aultman Health Care, OPW Fueling Components, Royal Thai Government, the Federal Aviation Administration (FAA), the Environmental Protection Agency (EPA), Microsoft, Premera Blue Cross Oregon, and the City of Seattle. She holds a Bachelor of Science in Behavioral Sciences from the University of Maryland and a Master of Fine Arts from Goddard College. Lisa lives in Houston, Texas, with her husband Bill, cats Paris and Siam, and dogs Hazel and Max.

To learn more about Lisa's work, visit:

Lisa Haneberg: www.lisahaneberg.com
Management Craft Blog: www.managementcraft.com

About TPH

You've got ideas. You have a proven track record. You want to share your success. But, how? We can help.

Who We Are

We are experienced training & development publishers who have spent more than 30 years working in the workplace, learning, & development industry. We have the expertise and professional contacts to take your winning ideas and turn them into respected, go-to training & development resources.

What We Do

We publish smart, engaging, and effective training & development content, providing expertise and support throughout the publishing process:

- Proposal review
- Content editing
- Book cover and interior design & layout
- Production—print and ebooks
- Subsidiary rights facilitation

How to Get Started

Send us your proposal, and we'll be in touch to get the ball rolling:

http://www.trainerspublishinghouse.com/contact-us.html

Trainers Publishing House
www.trainerspublishinghouse.com

About TPH

You've got ideas. You have a proven track record. You want to share your success. But, how? We can help.

Who We Are

We are experienced training & development publishers who have spent more than 30 years working in the workplace, learning, & development industry. We have the expertise and professional contacts to take your winning ideas and turn them into respected, go-to training & development resources.

What We Do

We publish smart, engaging, and effective training & development content, providing expertise and support throughout the publishing process:

- Proposal review
- Content editing
- Book cover and interior design & layout
- Production—print and ebooks
- Subsidiary rights facilitation

How to Get Started

Send us your proposal, and we'll be in touch to get the ball rolling:

http://www.trainerspublishinghouse.com/contact-us.html

Trainers Publishing House
www.trainerspublishinghouse.com

Made in the USA
San Bernardino, CA
11 June 2014